EDNA'S DIARY

ABOUT THE AUTHOR

Edna Page was born in Sandwich, Kent, in 1920, and lived there all her life. During World War Two she was in a reserved occupation as the manageress of a store in a large grocery chain. In 1947 she married ex-Marine Commando Denis Miles. In the 1950s she trained and worked as a Cordon Bleu chef. In the 1960s she retrained as an employment officer, eventually becoming Assistant Manager of Ramsgate Job Centre. After retiring in 1985, she was active in local voluntary causes. She died in 2009.

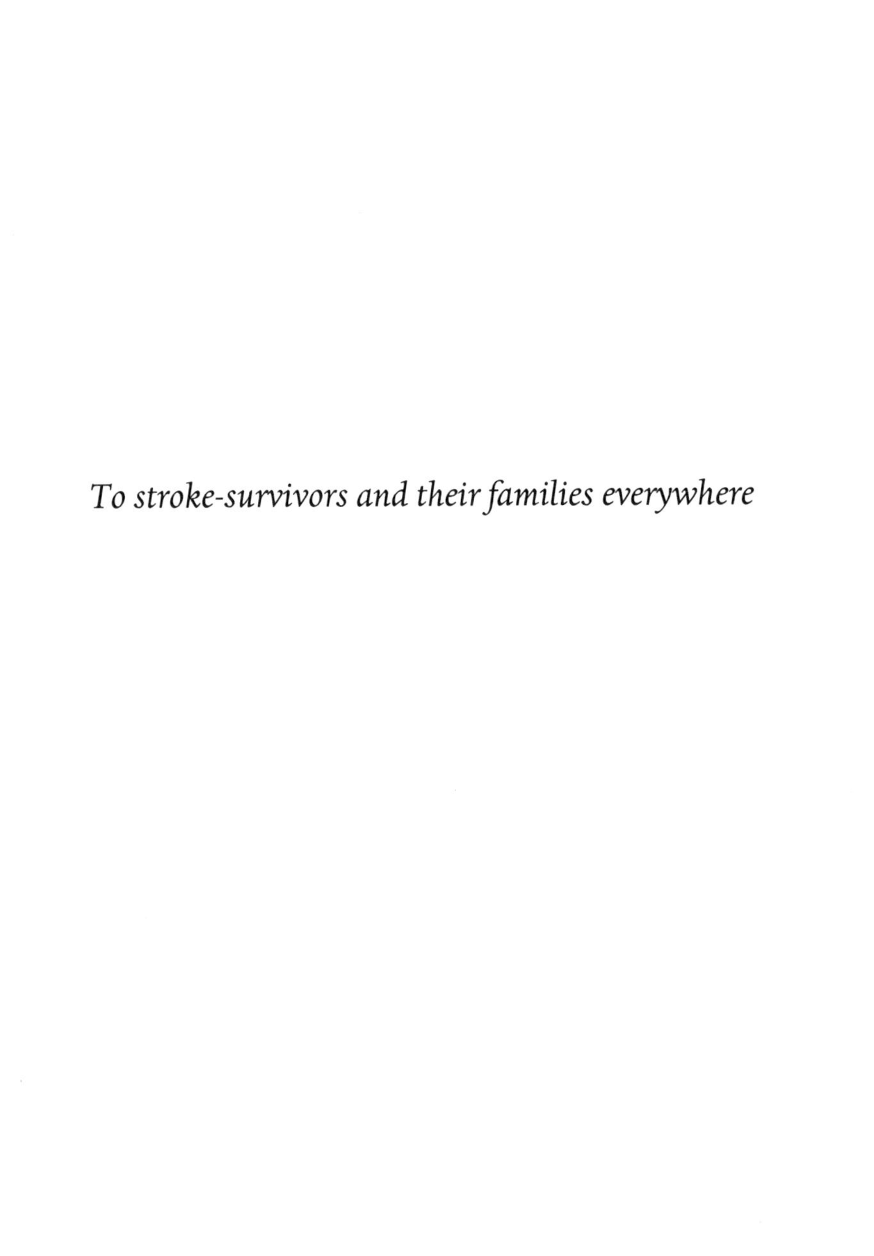

To stroke-survivors and their families everywhere

Photograph by E. Reisfeld

Edna Miles
(1958)

EDNA MILES

EDNA'S DIARY

Writing again after Stroke

Compiled by Patrick Miles

All proceeds from publication donated to Stroke Association UK

Sam&Sam
Cambridge

First published in 2021
by Sam&Sam
29 Highfield Avenue
Cambridge CB4 2AJ
www.samandsam.co.uk

Typeset in Dante MT by James Miles

British Library Cataloguing-in-Publication Data
A catalogue record for this book is available from the British Library

ISBN 978 1 9999676 3 5

Printed and bound by Amazon

2 4 6 8 10 9 7 5 3 1

CONTENTS

'Mini-memories'

Introduction

I hope you will enjoy this little book of selections from my mother Edna Miles's diary. You will find laughter and sadness here, and every subject under the sun – from her daily life and cooking, her friends, anecdotes, news and views, to the Royal Family, politics, wildlife, television, the NHS, and gardens.

But perhaps the most remarkable thing is that the ten thick volumes (335,000 words) from which I have made this selection were **all written after she had had a stroke**, and she had never written a diary in her life before…

My mother suffered a stroke on Christmas Eve 2002. She had a cerebral embolism on the left side of her brain and most of all this affected her communication: she was left with only 20% of her language faculty. She began language therapy at an NHS hospital in January 2003 and made good progress, but she couldn't write continuous prose. Just over a year later her therapist wrote in my mother's exercise book: 'Keep a diary. You don't need to write everything, just sometimes. Write about something you did/someone you saw. Don't write more than a paragraph.'

From a few, laborious lines, the diary she wrote from April 2004 really took off. She wrote it every day for the next five years. Eventually the whole town knew about 'Edna's Diary'!

There is no doubt that the diary helped her re-learn how to communicate. Because of her form of aphasia, she tended to express herself in short, simple sentences. Now she had to get these out onto the page, and this highlighted her problems. Her therapist addressed my mother's language problems through her diary; she helped make the diary more interesting; and friends of my mother's 'corrected' it with her. In January 2005 a computer assessed my mother as having achieved 89% language recovery and the sessions with her wonderful therapist ended.

Another benefit was that writing the diary the day after the events helped my mother's short-term memory, which had also been affected by the stroke. She would lay yesterday's newspaper beside her so that she could see that date and day of the week clearly (after her stroke she had great difficulty with numbers), and then write these out in her diary and describe that day's goings on. This became a ritual – so it helped her structure her day and manage her time, which was also a good thing.

Above all, we her family were so pleased that despite her stroke she had found something new and absorbing to do. It involved her with **people**, who read it, listened to her reading it, discussed it with her, or featured in it themselves. We enjoyed reading it tremendously and it's left us with an enduring record of 'who' she was, because we find it so alive and typical of her.

As Edna's son, then, I can thoroughly recommend keeping a diary as you recover from a stroke, as well as writing down 'mini-memories' like the ones I have included at the back of the book. Writing like this is not only therapeutic for the stroke-survivor, it can have all sorts of positive outcomes for others: family, descendants who never knew you, perhaps even future historians.

The front cover gives you an idea of the diary as it was written (any faint brown marks are Tippex). I have sometimes adjusted my mother's punctuation and supplied a note in brackets.

Good luck with your own writing!

Patrick Miles

Edna's Diary

Beginnings

1st April 2004. I went to Age Concern. Eric was there. I asked him if he had seen a parrot flying in the trees. I just said, 'April Fool.' He wasn't very amused!

(The first entry in the diary; it took Edna over an hour to write.)

Cheating slightly

2nd April 2004. Patrick and the family came back from Cornwall. They had a very good time. The weather was sunny most of the time. They saw Northern Summer House. The earliest structure in the gardens, this charming building was discovered without a roof at the end of 1991, completely engulfed by laurel. They arrived in Cambridge about 4 p.m.

(The sentence about 'this charming building' was Edna cheating! She had copied it from a postcard we sent her of Heligan, but her language therapist rumbled her and told her she must use her own words.)

Daily life may seem boring, then –

3rd July 2004. I had a very busy day. I did a fairly large wash. It was quite good for drying clothes. Everything dried in half an hour. So I ironed, but this took more, as I had 3 shirts, and 2 pairs of trousers and other bits and pieces to do. I watched the Tennis. It was very exciting. In the evening I cooked a plaice, tomatoes, shredded cabbage, and new potatoes. I finished with strawberries and yoghurt. Suddenly, at about 6 o'clock, Carol two doors away rang and said, 'Don't go outside, Edna!' She had to get someone to take a swarm of bees in her yew tree.

10th April 2004. I went across from Patrick's house in Cambridge to look after the house and fish while the owners were on holiday. I was surprised to hear a growling noise. It came from an alarm made in a large gnome in the hall.

3rd October 2005. I had my lunch at 1 o'clock. I cooked 2 filets of chicken, with lemon and garlic and vegetables. I ironed the clothes, and put them in the airing cupboard. I went across to see Ivy and we watched a cookery presentation called Dine With Me. The demonstrator showed how to cook OSTRICH!

'There's nowt so queer as folk'

30th July 2004. David wears shorts to drive the bus at Age Concern when it is very hot. I think they suit him. He is tall and they are very smart. But some people have complained. So now he has some new ones, which look rather baggy.

5th February 2006. Audrey told me that they had a Christmas card from Perce Walters. It showed a picture of the British Legion home where he is now living. He indicated by an arrow where the Bar is situated.

10th June 2006. My eighty-sixth birthday. Patrick did the shopping and met Muriel at the Co-op, so they came home together in her car. She is the same age as me. In the window of her car she has a sticker that says: 'Better to be an old fart than a young dickhead!'

'Empathy'

1st March 2005. At 12.15 I went to Age Concern for lunch. Geoffrey and Mary were there, and Richard. Richard doesn't usually sit with us. He is a small man with a humpback. He lives on his own. He has epilepsy. During lunch he had two small spasms, and fell, dropping his lunch over the table. He said he would clear it up, but Geoffrey knew that Richard would find it very difficult. I used to think Geoffrey a bit stuck up. But I must say I admired how quickly quietly [*sic*] he managed the situation.

31st May 2005. I went to Age Concern about 9.45 a.m. Maggie was on the desk. I asked her about her grandson Alex. I had a chat with Kath, and had a tea. Went to the Fruit Bowl and bought 2 oranges, 2 lemons, 2 bananas, and some spring greens. I walked round by the church. I noticed that the door was open into the Secret Garden. I saw a woman and a man, they asked me if the church was open. So I took them into the garden, they were surprised how beautiful everything was, I told them how to find Alan, at the Fruit Bowl, who will get a key to open the church. I told the man that the Curfew still rings at 8 p.m. He asked me, why? I got it a little mixed up. I told him I'll get it right in a moment, which I did. I told them that it was to call in the pigs in [*sic*] for the night. In Sandwich there is a place called Hogs Corner. I told him a few other things about Sandwich. I told him that once I had a stroke. He was very interested, because he was a doctor, and did understand about the therapy I had done. He and his wife went on their way to get the key from Alan.

A national event

9th April 2005. Helen rang about 9.30 a.m. She wanted to know if she could join me for a snack at lunch time, so that we could watch the wedding of Charles and Camilla together. To celebrate the Day, we started with a glass of sherry. Camilla wore a beautiful pale pink suit. At 2.30 all the Royals and some guests went to St George's Chapel for the blessing of the marriage. This was conducted by the Archbishop of Canterbury, Dr Rowan Williams. The blessing was very moving. The Archbishop wore a plain surplice. Helen said she would think he could have worn a better one. I must admit some of the other priests wore finer robes. I remarked to Helen that the Archbishop is a humble man.

A short story

20th April 2005. I got up early today. Started the washing. Rose came in, she told me that Jack attacked her (by the way Jack is one of her pet ducks). She has had them for two years, the other one is called Jemima. Actually I think she is getting fed up with them. She said, perhaps the RSPCA would like them. I suggested apple sauce would be better.

23rd April 2005. Rose knocked on the door. She asked me to lend her the fishing net. She is giving the ducks to Wingham Bird Park. I knew she was getting fed up with them.

24th April 2005. I got up about 8.45 a.m. I saw Rose over the hedge, she was looking for the ducks. Angie and Kevin were there (Kevin is Angie's new boyfriend). They caught Jack very quickly, but Jemima decided to run and fly away. Eventually Kevin caught her with the fishing net. He put the ducks inside a sack, and then transported them to Wingham Bird Park. Rose, Angie and Kevin watched them swim away. They were very happy in the stream, and then sitting on the bank.

A lady of firm views

26th December 2004. Everyone enjoyed the Boxing Day meal. N.B. I was quite surprised about Roderick. He has expanded so much. He eats more than his wife and brother and is rather round. He says he does not drink alacocohol [*sic*], but he made a hole in the brandy butter and trifle.

9th January 2005. It was a very windy day. However, I went for a walk and saw Janet Smith. We talked about the pantomime which we saw with Age Concern at the local theatre. We agreed it was rotten.

4th October 2005. Jean and I went to NADFAS. The lecture was given by Dr Dominic Purefoy. He is a monk. He was talking about the structure of worship and attitudes in a monastery. He was rather long-winded.

Personal

23rd January 2006. My husband Denis died 19 years ago today. He is always near me.

A memory

15th May 2006. I had my breakfast about 8.15 a.m. The weather was rather overcast. I read some of the newspaper. I noticed that some women are having their babies at home. Rather than going into hospital. When I was aged 28 years, I decided to have my baby at home. I was told by Dr Jones that if anything went wrong I would have to go to the Hospital. Everything went very well. Denis was then working on Drew's Farm as the carpenter. I got his breakfast, then everything started. I went in to Mrs Field's. So she went to Nurse Stacey. She was a wonderful nurse. Denis came to see me at 11 o'clock and Nurse Stacey asked him to go back to work. Then Mrs Drew phoned Mr Drew, and Mr Drew found Denis to say that he has a son. Nurse Stacey delivered Patrick before Dr Jones arrived. Dr Jones wasn't very pleased to see that Bindle my cocker spaniel was in the room most of the time and growled at him.

Age Concern the soap opera

10th August 2004. Today the bus came from Age Concern at 9.20 a.m. Usually it is about 10.30. Some people were going to an outing. They were going to the Special Breeds Farm, near to Maidstone. All the local people arrived at Age Concern, but the second bus broke down near Nonington. David was not able to get it to go. It was full of passengers. Some of them were unable to walk unless they were helped by the lift at the back of the bus. Several taxis came from Sandwich to Nonington and brought them to the Sandwich Centre. Some of the taxis had lifts. Eventually all of the passengers who were going to the outing were seated on a bus from another company. Alice and I did not go to the Outing. We had our lunch at Age Concern and went home at 2.30 p.m. – by taxi.

12th October 2004. I went early to Age Concern. I talked to Helen. She told me about two men who came to her door saying they are from the Water Board. She asked them in. They took her purse, but fortunately she was able to yell for her carer next door. The policeman came. Helen's neighbour was not so lucky. The men took some money from him.

11th October 2005. I arrived at Age Concern about 10.10 a.m. and chatted with people. Margery Whitton said that she had a present from the local Grammar School students for Harvest Festival. The gift included 3 rusty tins of vegetables, 2 onions, and 3 bananas. She asked me for the school's address. I was able to give it, as I had just written to them to thank them for what they sent me.

Local news

26th April 2004. After I went to Age Concern, I went to [see] Ivy. She told me that the W.I. are finishing trading at the market on the 27th of May. It has become very difficult to find helpers. Lots of people want to buy produce, but the helpers are in their seventies or eighties. And there are not many younger people who can find the time to help the stall. The women are all working.

(At nearly every stroke club I spoke to about my mother's Diary people discussed this entry.)

20th May 2006. I had my breakfast at about 8.15 a.m. It was a good day. I kept up with my Diary. Had a look at the *East Kent Mercury*. A whale was washed up on the breakwater at Kingsdown beach. It weighed 27 tonnes. Helen came to see me about 12.45 a.m., she brought me a pair of fawn socks from the Market. Steve, from the fishmongers at the Market, was selling steaks of OSTRICH.

8th November 2006. The doctor came to see me about 4 p.m. He had a red face. I suspect he has High Blood Pressure.

9th December 2008. A cold dreary day. There are two Christmas chrysanths out in the greenhouse.

Wildlife

18th February 2006. Helen said, her garden had been disturbed during the night. She picked up several pots and plants, she thought it was a dog who did it.

19th February 2006. It wasn't a dog who disturbed her garden, it is Badgers. Today it was worse than yesterday.

21st February 2006. I rang Helen, she told me that she has still got the Badgers in her garden. The gardener is bricking up the hole to keep them out.

10th March 2006. P.S. Helen said that the Badgers have been in her garden again. Now they have really dug some of it up.

15th March 2006. Helen told me that she thinks everything is going wrong with her house, but she has a cleaner in, and carer, and the carer's husband helps a lot. She looked at my Diary, and then she cheered up.

19th March 2006. Hilda picked me up at 2.15 p.m. to go to Helen's at Tilmanstone. Helen was on about the Badgers again.

20th March 2006. Helen came to see me. She says the Badgers are still ruining her garden.

5th April 2006. It was a very good day, but rather cold. I had a look at the newspaper. I noticed that people are wanting to cull Badgers. I think Helen will be pleased.

2nd June 2006. Ivy came across, she brought me a wholemeal loaf. We had tea, and watched Countdown, and then chatted. She told me that she is staying at her son Roger's for almost 2 weeks. One thing she is going to do is to visit the large Cat which her family are giving her for her Birthday. She doesn't yet know if it will be a Tiger or a Lion, but her sons paid for it to eat for a year.

2nd May 2005. I forgot to record that yesterday, while I was at Hilda's, I heard the cuckoo for the first time this year. The First of May. I heard it before the others did. Somehow it made us very happy.

My refrain

24th October 2006. I kept up with my Diary...

'You can't get away from politics'

14th November 2006. The War at Iraq is still on. The first woman soldier has been killed in Southern Iraq.

3rd October 2006. At the Conservative Conference in Bournemouth, David Cameron said that Brussels was too powerful.

23rd November 2006. I noticed that KGB defector Alexander Litvinenko died yesterday. It was suspected radiation poisoning that killed him.

30th December 2006. I read that Saddam Hussein is going to be hanged today.

23rd April 2007 (St George's Day). I noticed that Yeltsin died yesterday. The headlines say that he was a drunk who rescued Russia from Communist tyranny.

11th January 2008. I read in the paper that Gordon Brown has left Britain open to a cash crisis.

6th March 2008. I noticed that Gordon Brown said that I.D. cards must be free. So they should be.

22nd September 2008. I see that Gordon Brown has flown to New York, because Wall Street is in more chaos than he thought it was.

5th November 2008. Today History was made because the first black man was elected President of the United States. His name is Barack Obama.

A full day

7th December 2006. It was a very rainy windy day. I had my breakfast about 8.30. Ivy rang me to say that when

Enid's carer came to see her, she found Enid at the bottom of the stairs. The ambulance came, Ivy rang Enid's daughter, who followed the ambulance to hospital. I washed my hair. For my lunch I had a bacon sandwich. Ivy told me that when she was going to the Congregational church for coffee, she saw a friend fall over. A lorry carrying girders pushed her in the road. The ambulance came and Ivy rang her friend's son, who followed it in his car. I watched 'Flog It', for my supper I had cold salmon with salad and a baked potato, I finished with prunes and ice cream. At 8.00 I watched 'The Queen's Lost Uncle'. It was about Prince George, Duke of Kent. He was married to Princess Marina. Patrick rang to say that Frank was a little better.

(See the section below, 'Cousin Frank'.)

'A Festival of Trees'

9th December 2006. At about 3 p.m. Patrick and I went to St Peter's Church to look at the 'Festival of Trees'. There were 45 decorated trees in the church. They looked wonderful. There will be three prizes for the best ones. It was £2 to see the Christmas trees. The money collected is to go to the St Clement's Tower appeal. I think the idea of the Festival was excellent. Patrick, Ivy and I spoke to lots of people as we were having tea and mince pies. There must have been a lot of work to organise it. We got home about 5 p.m.

Cousin Frank

10th December 2006. Patrick rang me about 9.30 p.m. to say that Frank had died. He was my cousin, and also my friend. He will be greatly missed. He and I used to play together when we lived in St Peter's Street. I remember when I was eleven years old and he was only six, I coaxed him to go with me to Dover to visit our Aunt Rachel. He rode a fairy cycle and I rode a small bicycle. We eventually arrived at Dover. I had promised him a toy at Woolworth's, so I bought it. Unfortunately, we never got to Aunt Rae's. It was then getting very late, so we biked back to Sandwich. We were met by my Mum and Dad. They were looking for us and we had got almost to Eastry. My mother picked up Frank and the fairy cycle, and took them with my Dad in the car, to go home to Sandwich. My mother told me to ride home to Sandwich, which I did. I had a telling off.

Christmas in Cambridge 2006

25th December 2006. It was a dull day, but in the house it was very warm and comfortable. We all greeted everyone with Happy Christmas! We had breakfast about 8.30 then went to church to the 10.00 a.m. service. The church was decorated, although there weren't a lot of people in the congregation. Unfortunately, the organist was ill. At the last minute, a lady played the carols etc on the piano. I must say the church had a very warm feeling about it. The sermon was excellent, it was about how Christmas cards have stopped printing the Nativity on the front as they used to, so they have lost the message about Families. We then came home and opened our presents. I had some wonderful ones: a pair of slippers, a bottle of perfume, two new diaries, chocolate, a pot of honey, pot of ginger in syrup, notelets, biscuits etc. During the day, several family and friends rang to say Happy Christmas. We had a magnificent feast of turkey in the evening. It was a very excellent Christmas Day.

Boxing Day, 26th December 2006. I kept up with my Diary, then about 11.00 a.m. we went by car to Wicken Fen. It was a bit foggy and there were quite a lot of people visiting. Ally had hired a wheelchair. I walked some of the time, but found that the wheelchair helped me see more things. It was good to see the countryside. We had a drink at a pub. We got home about one o'clock. We had mushroom soup, with bread, salad, cheese straws, and cheese and fruit. Then we watched the ballet on television at Covent Garden, 'Giselle', one of the best ballets. After that, we watched 'Dad's Army'. It was a repeat, but I had not seen it before. It was about the veterans giving a Christmas turkey dinner to the old citizens.

(Ally is my wife.)

27th December 2006. At 2 p.m. we went to see 'Snow White' on ice at the Cambridge Corn Exchange. The skating and dancing was tremendous. The acting was also terrific. It was presented by the Wild Rose Company from Russia. All the artistes were also jugglers and acrobats. During the twenty minutes interval we had ice creams. It really was a good show. There were several people sitting in wheelchairs. We got home about 5 p.m.

('Snow White' was produced by Vee Deplidge and choreographed by Giuseppe Arena.)

Weathers

18th January 2007. It was a very windy day. The ferries didn't go. Several people were killed by trees. One man was crushed in his car. Gale force winds were in Brighton, and there was a blanket of snow in Scotland. Rose came in. She told me that the wind had blown her over.

21st July 2007. The floods in Tewkesbury are awful. Some people were saved by a helicopter. I rang Gurney at Bredon to ask how he managed. He told me that he just got home before the clouds opened, then it rained for an hour. He told me that several of his neighbours were under water. He told me that his dairy was flooded, so he wasn't able to get any milk. He thanked me for ringing.

(Gurney is my father-in-law.)

Newspaper nuggets

4th January 2007. The *Daily Mail* says there could be a plague of rats because the rubbish is now collected fortnightly.

6th February 2007. I noticed that it was reported that Bird Flu has hit Bernard Matthews farms in Sussex and 10,000 turkeys have been slaughtered.

10th February 2007. The headlines are about the Bird Flu. The big question is, 'Does it harm humans?' Probably it doesn't. But I think most people are being careful and avoiding shops that sell turkey meat.

26th February 2007. I noticed that Helen Mirren has been given a BAFTA as Best Actress for playing the Queen. I have seen bits of the film. It looked excellent. I think the Queen herself was very pleased with Helen Mirren's portrayal of her.

20th April 2007. I kept up with my Diary, and read the newspaper. I noticed that British Gas is fiddling the bills, especially for the customers who pay by direct debit.

6th August 2007. I read that there is another Foot and Mouth Outbreak. (I think it is terrible news.)

14th August 2007. I read some of the newspaper. I noticed that a police chief has called for the legal drinking age to be raised to 21, also that care homes are dreadful.

16th October 2007. It is reported that obesity is deadlier than smoking.

27th August 2008. I did some cleaning in the kitchen, then read some of the newspaper. I noticed that dark chocolate is very good for you when eaten moderately.

Three mothers

31st July 2007. I went for a short walk. I met Sheila and Lynn. They live next door to each other. It was quite interesting listening to them. Both of them have children attending a special school. Because the children are disabled, their husbands cleared off. Sheila manages very well. Her mother helps her almost every day, and the DHSS have given her a small car to take her son out. He is about 17 years old now, and a very large boy. Lynn's son is younger, about 12 I think. He goes to school Monday-Friday, but Lynn looks after him at weekends. Sheila is a nice-looking woman about 48 years old. Lynn is a large good-looking woman aged about 35. I think both of them are very brave to manage so well.

(As generally in the Diary, names here have been changed.)

Incident with a starling

15th March 2007. Rose told me that yesterday she had a bird in her chimney. Naturally, it was trapped. The Council sent a man to release it. It flew away – it was a starling. When the man looked at the gas fire, he said it wasn't connected right. The gas fire had a leak. The man said, that bird probably saved Rose's life (she said it was 'meant to be'). Rose knew the man who installed the gas fire, a Mr Burford from Hopton. The man from Canterbury is making a complaint, because Mr Burford said he was a Corgi fitter.

The daily walk

14th June 2007. I went for a short walk. I couldn't help noticing how polite the children are, playing outside their houses. Some of them said hello in a friendly way.

30th August 2008. I bumped into Evelyn Barton on my walk. I haven't seen her for ages. She told me that many years ago I helped her and her husband negotiate when they were buying their own council house. I reminded her that she used to help with the cleaning when Gran lived with us after having a bad stroke.

('Gran' here is Edna's mother, Maria Page (1891-1982))

Television titbits

5th December 2006. I watched Heston Blumenthal cooking roasted chicken. It was a disastrous failure. I then watched half of 'Ramsay's Kitchen', which was very interesting.

13th January 2007. Patrick and I watched 'When We Were Scouts'. I used to be a Girl Guide. I was in the Kingfisher's pack. In the Brownies I was a sprite.

21st January 2008. In the evening I watched 'Mastermind' and 'University Challenge'. Jeremy Paxman was in the news yesterday because he complained about Marks & Spencer pants (they are too skimpy).

14th May 2008. I watched 'Children of Our Time'. It was about children aged between 7-14 and how they manage the stresses of life, e.g. bullying and exams. It was extremely interesting.

3rd June 2008. I watched 'Spring Watch', which was excellent. The other day Simon King identified the droppings of animals – the easy one was the Cat's.

30th September 2008. I watched 'Jamie's Ministry of Food'. It was very good, but I don't think Jamie Oliver enhanced it by swearing.

Tea with a neighbour

30th August 2007. Mabel Petley rang me to invite me to her home to have tea with her. She lives just round the corner. She was very pleased to see me. She laid on a good tea, with cake, toasted muffins etc. I put on a fresh top, thank goodness, because she was all dolled up. It reminded me of when my Gran used to take tea with Mrs Ovenden in the 1920s and Gran used to put her hat on and gloves.

('Gran' here is Edna's grandmother, Elizabeth Beck (1866-1945); for more about this occasion see 'Mini-memories'.)

Appliances...

31st July 2008. When the nurse came to dress my leg, she discovered there was no hot water in the tap. She managed with the kettle. I rang Patrick in Cambridge. He contacted the gas man (Terry), who fixed it. It seems that the pilot had gone out because it was clogged with ant powder. Then the man had to come from TV Rentals to replace the television! It is the same as the old one and I'm very pleased with it.

A taste of France

3rd October 2007. I watched 'Coronation Street', then 'The Restaurant'. I thought it was very interesting. There are only three couples left. To tempt customers, one couple held a wine tasting day in their restaurant and gave one glass of champagne free. The second couple had two attractive girls entertaining by doing the cancan. The ladies who were eating there were not amused, but the men were delighted.

The garden

2nd February 2008. It was a sunny cold day. The other day I noticed that there were some snowdrops and early Irises out. When Patrick looked at the garden, he noticed that there was a bush of pink winter Daphne out, in a pot. It was really beautiful, and the fragrance was heavenly. It was planted six years ago from a cutting.

The Royal Family

5th March 2007. I see that there's trouble about Diana, again. The inquest is coming up at last. I feel very sorry for Harry and William, they can never forget about the tragedy. It is almost 10 years since Diana died.

15th April 2007. I watched Andrew Marr. He reported that Prince William is now flirting with 2 other well-connected young women. So the engagement of William and Kate Middleton is on hold, at the time.

17th April 2007. It says in the newspaper that William is horrified at sneers about Kate Middleton's mother. It seems that Kate isn't good enough to marry William. At the palace they say that Mrs Middleton was just an air stewardess and her husband an airline pilot. Actually I think the Royals are just SNOBS. Kate has got over William very well. She's a beautiful girl, and will be her own woman.

1st October 2007. I notice that the inquests of Diana and Dodi Fayed start today. Paul Burrell, her butler, is a Key Witness.

6th October 2007. I noticed in the newspaper that Wills and Kate are together again. Also that there isn't going to be an Election after all. It seems Gordon Brown got cold feet.

14th December 2007. The newspaper is full about the death of Diana and Dodi. I think it was true that Diana was a rather silly girl, but I don't think Charles is so clever either. In my opinion, Diana would have been happy had it not been for the affair between Charles and Camilla.

2nd August 2008. I notice that Will (Prince) is now living next to Charles and Camilla – does that mean that the engagement between Will and Kate is postponed?

In memoriam

7th July 2007. I kept up with my Diary, then Patrick and I met Hilda and we all went into a taxi to go to Deal, and have lunch at No. 47 Beach Street. Helen, Hilda and I used to eat together often. Sadly, Helen isn't with us any more. She died almost a year ago. So I thought it would be a good idea to celebrate our meetings together. We had a toast to Helen. She would have enjoyed our meal. We all recalled some of the things which Helen used to do and talk about. Hilda said that Helen was a very private person. Patrick read two or three letters which she had sent him. I remember that she was a warm, considerate person. We will always remember her with love. It was a lively happy lunch.

My refrain

10th January 2008. I brought my diary to date...

Getting things in perspective

14th July 2008. I had my breakfast about 8.30 a.m. Then the milkman came, and I paid him. He has been grumbling about the flowers, which grow beside the path to the front door. When it is warm, he wears shorts, but the flowers scratch his legs. I said, 'I'm sorry, but I can't do anything about it.' He then apologised and said, 'I'm grumbling about nothing.' Actually I couldn't help laughing to myself.

Memories

12th August 2008. I had a go at the crossword, but didn't get very far. I had a rest, then did some of my Journal. I have written some of what I used to do when I was at school.

15th August 2008. Peter Wilson came to see me. He gave me a box of Roses chocolates. We chatted together. He made a cup of tea and I cut two slices of Victoria sponge. I was very pleased to see Peter. I told him that I am trying to do more of my Journal. I showed him some of it – I asked him if he would correct any mistakes – he did a good job of it.

17th August 2008. Hilda came to see me, we chatted together. She brought about 6 paintings to show me, which she painted at her Art class. I thought they were excellent. I liked the painting which she made of spring flowers best. I showed her a bit of my Journal. As she paints, so I attempt to write interesting things which happened years ago.

26th September 2008. Had a go at the crossword. I sat down and wrote an episode of my Journal. I was very slow, but I wrote for an hour.

(Edna's 'Journal' is a collection of 'mini-memories' – see below.)

Medical

8th November 2008. I took three pills, but I had taken them earlier. Patrick is on holiday in Norfolk. So I rang Chris, Ivy's daughter-in-law. Eventually I went to Margate Hospital to check if I was all right. I went in an ambulance. I had some tests. Chris and Ivy joined me about 2.30 p.m. I had several checks – for my heart, blood pressure etc. Chris and Ivy stayed with me all the time. Eventually I got home, the time was 7 p.m. I must say, Chris and Ivy were wonderful. Ivy slept in my house last night.

Nurses

13th February 2008. Dawn came to dress my leg. She has 4 grown up children. She is now working half time. She is going to help her daughter, who is a nurse. Her daughter has one baby aged 9 months, and is expecting another. So she has her hands full. Dawn told me that when she was young she used to pick up potatoes, and other vegetables. The farmer paid his workers well. I told her I also used to pick up potatoes etc.

14th April 2008. Jean, the nurse, came to dress my leg. She told me that she is retiring next week. She is aged 68 years. She has been half-time for several years. I shall miss her, she is a very caring, proficient nurse. She is very good at juggling, and now is showing her grandchildren how to juggle – she has six grandchildren.

2nd May 2008. Emma came to dress my leg. I asked her how she did with her exams. She got 100%. I then asked her how her father was. She told me that sadly he died on his birthday. He was aged 82 years old. I was very sorry to hear it. She gave me another different pad on my leg.

19th May 2008. At 9 a.m., Dawn the Nurse came to dress my leg. I haven't seen her for five weeks. She told me that her daughter has a new baby. It is a girl, she is called Maisie, and weighs 6 lb 6 oz. Dawn was delighted. She told me that my leg is much better.

21st July 2008. I kept up with my diary. Then Lindy the Nurse came to dress my leg. I get on very well with her.

She has been away for 3 weeks on holiday with her husband. I asked her when she is getting her new dog. She replied, 'Next week.' She is calling him Murphy. I said, 'I thought you were calling him Spud.' He is 8 weeks old. So she is having 3 weeks off to train him. She said it would be a good idea if I saw someone about the fungi on my toes.

25th August 2008. Dawn the Nurse came to dress my leg. She told me that my skin is rather dry. She told me that she is going to Margate Hospital to have one of her knees replaced. Actually, she fell down when she was lifting one of her patients. She will be away for 5 weeks. I'm very sorry for Dawn. I shall miss her enormously.

Food standards

30th November 2008. Denise came to see me and we chatted together. She told me that she had had Sunday lunch with a friend, they ate at 'Herbert's'. She said it was the worst meal she has had for ages. It was cold, the vegetables weren't cooked well, and the dessert wasn't good at all. So she will not go there again. Before that, she went to the Lifeboat Bazaar and bought some scones. We had 2 of them with our tea. She said, 'What do you think of them, Edna?' I replied, 'Well, they are quite nice, but not so good as you make.' (But they were stale.) She answered, 'They are the worst scones I've eaten.' I don't think it was her day, for eating food.

An interrogation

16th May 2007. Joan Parker rang me to invite me to tea. I declined. I told her I was very sorry, but I got very behind with my chores and Diary. She was talking to me quite a long time. She asked me if I had heard about my friend Helen's Will. She said: 'You did well!' I didn't retaliate. I was rather surprised, she told me that her friend Charles told her. I wasn't very pleased.

8th April 2009. Joan Parker came to see me. I think that she is rather nosy. We had tea together. She asked me if I would like to go to Wayfarers Care Home for 2 weeks – I declined. She is aged 77 years old. She asked me about my grandchildren. I answered her, 'They are doing very well.' She asked who does my cleaning. I deflected the question. She even asked me what I was having for my supper.

Brought to the table

12th May 2009. At 11.30 I started to eat Wiltshires meals-on-wheels. A man named Bob introduced himself. He was very pleasant. The lamb was excellent. I had lamb stew with fresh vegetables, and finished with a Bakewell tart. I then had a rest.

An afternoon jaunt

29th May 2009. It was the hottest day of the year. Patrick and I had breakfast about 8.45 a.m. For lunch we had fillets of salmon, with tomatoes, new potatoes, and baked apples. I had a rest. Patrick then pushed me to the Salutation. The gardens were beautiful. There were now lots of flowers out, mostly several varieties of Iris. At home I have quite a few of them. It took us about an hour at the gardens. Denis used to work there in his spare time. One of the features is a very interesting water garden. Then we had tea with Earl Grey and a very large slice of coffee sponge. Actually this is the first time I have been out since Christmas.

(The Salutation is a house designed by Sir Edwin Lutyens, with a garden inspired by Gertrude Jekyll.)

Life is still good

10th June 2009. Today is my birthday. I am aged 89. I opened my cards. I had fourteen. They were all very good, with pictures that I like. Rose came in to say 'happy birthday', she gave me some carnations and a bar of Bournville chocolate. Then Ivy came across, she said 'Happy birthday' and kissed me, and gave me a booklet about Sandwich. Patrick was the first to greet me, on the phone. He and the family sent me a very peaceful card, a green garden with trees etcetera. So I had a very good birthday. I kept up with my Diary.

Last entry

13th June 2009. It was a very hot day. Patrick and I ate about 8 a.m. Whilst he was here, I told him that Hilda sold one of her paintings for £10. It was the only one sold from her Art class. For lunch Patrick cooked fried fish, chips and peas. I had a rest. Patrick did some exam marking. Then Patrick went home. He rang me to say he got to Cambridge at 6 p.m. in the evening. I watched the Trooping of the Colour. The Queen looked fine. She wore a beautiful blue hat.

(Edna was taken ill next day and died in hospital on 19th June 2009.)

Mini-memories

My Gran

When I was aged 5 years, my Father and Mother decided that I should live at my Gran's (Elizabeth Beck, née Langford) in St Peter's Street, because it would be better for me to be educated in the Sandwich school. There I was quite happy. Uncle Jim, her son, lived in the back room. He worked as an engine driver. Everything was very comfortable, especially in the winter, when Gran used to light a small open fire – it was quite near to my bed. I liked Jim enormously. He used to sit downstairs in the large kitchen in a chair. He used to sing and hum in front of the fire there and two or three times a week I used to wash his feet. Gran used to sit in a small nursing chair, Gran used to hum and sing as well.

Formal Tea

My Gran was a very kind lady. She had beautiful long grey hair, which she put up in a bun. She was very slim with fine bones. She always wore black long skirts. When she went out she wore a bodice, which was made of grey silk. Even when we were invited to tea by her friend Mrs Ovenden, who lived ten doors away, she would wear a hat and gloves. She dressed me up in a clean dress, with white knee socks, and I wore black shoes with straps over my feet. There was my Gran and me sitting in Mrs Ovenden's sitting room sipping tea. Mrs Ovenden had some pretty cups and saucers, china I think. The ladies were chatting away, gossiping I expect! I kept fidgeting and looked round the room. There were some stuffed birds in a case. Mrs Ovenden had a granddaughter about two years older than me, but she had managed to get out of the tea party.

My best friend

My best friend was Edna Silk. She was just 2 years older than me. She lived two doors away with her mother and father, and 5 brothers and one other sister. They were a very happy family. We used to play in the street, sometimes whipping a top round and round. The whip was made of thin leather. Sometimes we skipped, with two older girls holding the rope across the road. Sometimes there were several children skipping together over the rope. We used to sing rhymes as we skipped. I also used to play with a diabolo. I could throw it over the telegraph wires and catch it. When the evenings closed in Edna and I sat round about the gaslight, watching Mr Mantle (that really was his name) putting the lights on in the street. After that, my Gran used to call me in. Usually she asked Edna also to come in. We both had something to eat. We would sit down and the oil lamp would give a good glow. Gran would be sitting in her nursing chair, which I am sure she had for years.

(A diabolo is a two-headed top which is thrown up and caught on a string between two sticks.)

Washing-day

Every Monday was washing-day. I used to get home from school about noon. The washing-shed was at the end of the garden, with a window facing the back of the house. In the shed there was a stone copper, which Gran lit quite early in the morning. The clothes were put into piles – whites, very grubby things, and colours, and last was Jim's overalls. There was a long bench, where the baths were. The hot water was put in them, then Gran and Aunt Rae rubbed the clothes vigorously. There was a 'posher', which was in a long tub. Then the clothes looked quite clean. When they were clean, the whites were blued, which is done with a cube of Reckitt's blue inside a cotton sack. Then it was my turn. I stood on a box and turned the mangle. I did it as quickly as I could, because I knew I was going to get my dinner. It was always mince, from Sunday's joint. By the way, Sunlight Soap was used to wash the clothes. Sunlight Soap came in yellow bars.

(A 'posher' was a washing-dolly. At my talks about Edna's Diary, everyone had their memories of Washing Day.)

The cinema, Sandwich

I remember the Cinema. I would be about 9 years old. Mr Claringbould bought it. His daughter was a friend of mine. I really only saw the front seats, as I only went to the matinees, on Saturdays at 2 p.m. There were only silent films then. There was a villain, a hero, and a heroine. The pictures flickered. Quite often the film broke down. There was a piano in the cinema, which was played by Mrs Langden, who lived next door to the cinema. She was a good pianist, but sometimes went too loud when she should be playing more softly. There was a gallery upstairs, but children never went there. Mr Potts used to come on Saturdays at 2 p.m. He was supposed to keep us in order. I'm sure he had a terrible job on his hands. Sometimes the film was boring. So some of us used to suck oranges. This made him mad. I understand that the Cinema was burned out before Mr Claringbould bought it.

A dangerous illness

When I was about 11 years old, I fell quite ill. Dr Hollands came to see me after one or two days. He told Gran I had got scarlet fever. There wasn't a fever hospital near and I was the only one to have it. So my Mother nursed me. The ambulance came, 2 men carried me out, and drove me to Cooper Street, Ash, where Mum and Dad lived. Everything was sterilised, with a sheet across the door. People were only to look at me from the window outside. I was ill for about six weeks. Mum was wonderful, she was with me all the time. Occasionally Dr Hollands came to see me. I'm sure one night I saw 2 Angels guarding me. The next day when Dr Hollands came he said to Mum, 'She's over the crisis.' Then I was eventually much better. I had several favourite toys whilst I was in bed, but they were all burned with other things. Then I came back to Gran's in Sandwich, but it was many weeks before I went to school because I was very afraid of everything.

(Two of my mother's aunts died of scarlet fever as children, and her sister Mary died of Spanish Flu in 1918.)

The errand girl

When I was aged 15 years old I worked as an apprentice florist at Miss Young's shop in Deal. I didn't like mossing wreaths because usually there were slugs in the moss. So for quite a while I was the errand girl. Two boxes were tied on my bicycle, I used to ride the length of Deal, and I used to lose my way. Soon I met the errand boys. That was quite fun. We used to race and do tricks with our bicycles. One boy had a hare lip, he was very good and used to help me find the addresses in Deal. Soon they knew me better and asked me to join their gang. There were about 7 boys and me. We used to sing on the pavement in front of the Queen's Hotel, which was rather grand. There was a special boy who could sing and dance better than any of us. His name was Norman Wisdom and he was the errand boy for the Maypole grocery stores. He didn't know me very much but I thought he was very clever. I would join with the others in the chorus and then Norman would give a signal that the Manager of the hotel was coming and in a blink of an eye we had all gone to our shops.

Printed in Great Britain
by Amazon

87113696R00027

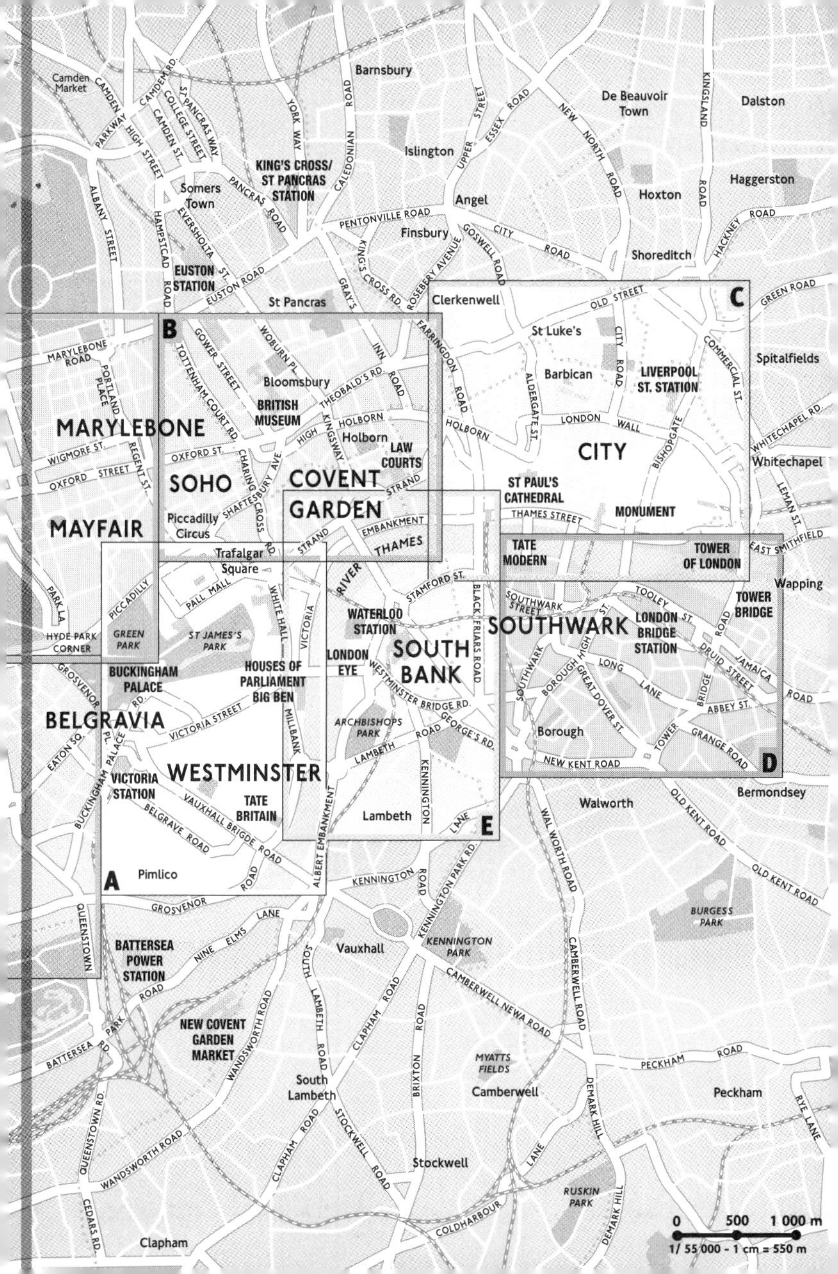
Camden Market
Barnsbury
De Beauvoir Town
Dalston
Islington
KING'S CROSS/ ST PANCRAS STATION
Somers Town
Angel
Hoxton
Haggerston
Finsbury
Shoreditch
EUSTON STATION
St Pancras
Clerkenwell
C
B
St Luke's
Spitalfields
Bloomsbury
Barbican
LIVERPOOL ST. STATION
BRITISH MUSEUM
MARYLEBONE
Holborn
LAW COURTS
CITY
Whitechapel
SOHO
COVENT GARDEN
ST PAUL'S CATHEDRAL
MONUMENT
MAYFAIR
Piccadilly Circus
Trafalgar Square
TATE MODERN
TOWER OF LONDON
Wapping
TOWER BRIDGE
WATERLOO STATION
SOUTHWARK
LONDON BRIDGE STATION
GREEN PARK
ST JAMES'S PARK
HYDE PARK CORNER
LONDON EYE
SOUTH BANK
BUCKINGHAM PALACE
HOUSES OF PARLIAMENT BIG BEN
BELGRAVIA
ARCHBISHOPS PARK
Borough
WESTMINSTER
VICTORIA STATION
TATE BRITAIN
Lambeth
E
D
Walworth
Bermondsey
A
Pimlico
BURGESS PARK
Vauxhall
KENNINGTON PARK
BATTERSEA POWER STATION
NEW COVENT GARDEN MARKET
MYATTS FIELDS
South Lambeth
Camberwell
Peckham
Stockwell
RUSKIN PARK
Clapham
RIVER THAMES
0
500
1 000 m
1/ 55 000 - 1 cm = 550 m

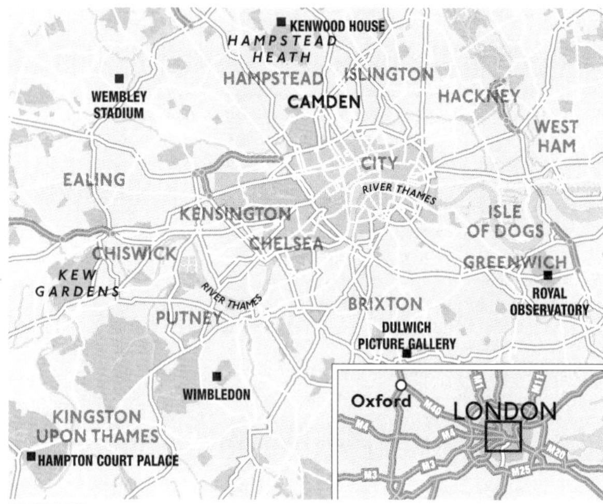

EXCURSIONS

Food
Spitalfields Market, see C.
Borough Market, see D.

SIGHTSEEING

By bus
The Original London Sightseeing Tour
→ *Tel. 020 8877 1722 £19 (£12 children); valid 24 hrs; www.theoriginaltour.com*
Guided tours in an open-top bus (get on and off wherever you like).
Enjaysee Tours
→ *Tel. 020 8906 8657 www.enjayseetours.com*
Tailor-made itineraries.
By boat
London River Service
→ *Tel. 020 7941 2400 www.tfl.gov.uk/river*
Boat trips on the Thames.
Jason's Trip
→ *Tel. 020 7222 1234 www.jasons.co.uk*
For a 90-minute journey down the canal from Little Venice to Camden.
Tate to Tate
→ *Tel. 020 7887 8888 £4 per journey*
Tate Britain to Tate Modern (or vice-versa) by boat, passing by the London Eye.
On foot
The Original London Walks
→ *Tel. 020 7624 3978 www.walks.com*
Over 100 guided group walks every week.

SPORTS

Epsom Downs
→ *Epsom (Surrey) Tel. 01372 470 047 From London Waterloo Station*
Londoners' favorite horse-racing course in the county of Surrey (the Oaks and the Derby are held in June).
Lords
→ *St John's Wood Rd, NW8 Tel. 020 7289 1611 Jubilee subway line; 90-minute guided tour*
The cricket pitch hosting the finals of the most important test matches.
Twickenham
→ *Whitton Rd, Twickenham; District subway line, stop at Richmond rail station Tel. 0870 143 1111*
The stronghold of rugby, where the Six Nations rugby matches are played from January to March.
Wimbledon Stadium
→ *Plough Lane; subway station: Tooting Broadway Tel. 0870 840 8905*
Greyhound races (Fri-Sat and Tue nights).

THE BEST VIEWS OF LONDON

→ From the eighth floor of the **Oxo Tower** (**E** C2)
→ From the highest observation wheel in the world, the **London Eye** (**E** B3)
→ From the dome of **St Paul's Cathedral** (**C** B3).
→ From **Primrose Hill**, north of Regent's Park.

EXCURSIONS

Hampstead Heath and Kenwood House
→ *Highgate subway station on the Northern line*
Magnificent Georgian house on Hampstead Heath, overlooking the city. Now a museum.
Kew Gardens
→ *Kew Rd; Kew Gardens station on the District line*
A wonderful 19th-century park and a UNESCO site. Japanese garden, green-houses and all varieties of flowers and trees.
Hampton Court Palace
→ *East Molesey, Surrey South West Trains; Hampton Court station; www.hrp.org.uk*
The palace of Henry VIII. Don't miss the Tudor kitchens and the world-famous maze.
Royal Observatory
→ *Greenwich Park; Docklands Light Railway; Cutty Sark station*
This observatory, built by Wren, is cut in half by the Greenwich meridian.
Dulwich Picture Gallery
→ *Gallery Rd, Dulwich Village; West Dulwich station, Orpington Line; www.dulwichpicture gallery.org.uk*
One of the most outstanding collections of European old masters (Poussin to Rembrandt).
Brighton
→ *50 minutes by train from Victoria rail station*
Londoners' seaside destination, with old Victorian promenades.
Oxford
→ *1½ hrs by train from Paddington rail station*
The most famous university town.

GNICO

RECKLESS RECORDS

HAMLEYS

tapas list intimidates. Last year the brothers opened a less formal small tapas bar nearby. Barrafina (54 Frith St; **B** A3) is always busy and there's a no-booking policy so it may be hard to find a free stool. Tapas around £5.

Yauatcha (**B** A3)
→ 15 Broadwick St
Tel. 020 7494 8888
Mon-Sat 8am–11.30pm; Sun 9am–10.30pm
Alan Yau's previous venture, Hakkasan (8 Hanway Place; **B** B3), had a brilliant design by Christian Liaigre (much copied thereafter) and excellent dim sum, for which it won a Michelin star. Yauatcha is another dim sum paradise with a dimly-lit downstairs dining room, a decor of luminous fish tanks and a modern, hip vibe throughout. The teahouse upstairs has 150 types of tea and the most gorgeous miniature cakes. Dim sum £3–6.

TEAROOM, BARS, MUSIC VENUES

Momo (**B** A4)
→ 25 Heddon St, W1
Tel. 020 7734 4040
Daily noon–midnight
Take a trip to North Africa with mint tea and all kinds of delicacies to tempt the sweet-toothed; comfy cushions, rugs and copper platters. You can also lunch next door.

Aperitivo (**B** A4)
→ 41 Beak St, W1
Tel. 020 7287 2057
Mon-Sat noon–11pm
Aperitivo's motto is 'To share is to enjoy'. It is an ideal meeting point after a tiring afternoon shopping in Soho. Good Italian-style tapas and good wine list.

Alphabet (**B** A4)
→ 61–63 Beak St, W1
Tel. 020 7439 2190
Mon-Sat noon–11pm
A popular bar with a map of Soho painted on the floor, comfy car seats doubling as armchairs and a laid-back feel to it. Cocktails, wine and beers.

Ronnie Scott's (**B** B3)
→ 47 Frith St, W1
Tel. 020 7439 0747
Daily 6pm–3am (midight Sun); book ahead; www.ronniescotts.co.uk
This legendary jazz club has attracted all the big names since it opened in 1959. Following a change of ownership the place was given a subtle make-over by Parisian designer Jacques Garcia (he of the Hotel Costes' Black Bar in Paris). The music hasn't changed – it's still great.

London Coliseum (**B** C4)
→ St Martin's Lane, WC2
Tel. 020 7632 8300
Cheap seats for same day shows on sale from 10am; www.eno.org
This symbol of the West End has a magnificent blue and gold original decor (1904), with public gallery spaces and a glass-roofed Terrace Bar. All the operatic works are sung in English.

SHOPPING

Milroy's of Soho (**B** B3)
→ 3 Greek St, W1
Tel. 020 7437 9311
Mon-Sat 10am–8pm (7pm Sat); tasting sessions by reservation until 11pm
Specialist whisky store whose cellar was once used to breed snails for L'Escargot restaurant down the road. With hundreds of different brands on sale, including Port Ellen and Dallas Dhu, it is heaven for connoisseurs.

Hamleys (**B** A4)
→ 188-196 Regent St, W1
Mon-Sat 10am–8pm (Sat 9am); Sun noon–6pm
Thousands of games and toys over six floors. Skilled demonstrations by staff. Beware of the maddening crowds of kids and their parents before Christmas.

Ray's Jazz Shop (**B** C3)
→ Foyle's, 113 Charing Cross Rd, WC2 Mon-Sat 9.30am–9pm; Sun noon–6pm
Ray's tiny shop is on the first floor of Foyle's bookstore, alongside an equally small but truly pleasant coffee shop. Very good selection of jazz CDs.

Berwick Street (**B** B3)
The street for small record stores: indie (**Sister Ray** at no. 34); second-hand (**Reckless Records** at no. 26); electronic (**Vinyl Junkies** at no. 94); everything (**Mr CD** at no. 80).

Murder One (**B** C4)
→ 76/78 Charing Cross Rd, WC2 Tel. 020 734 3483
Mon-Sat 10am–7pm
This excellent crime and mystery bookstore also sells out-of-print and secondhand editions.

Liberty (**B** A3)
→ 214 Regent St, W1
Mon-Sat 10am–8pm (9pm Thu; 7pm Sat); Sun noon–6pm
Begun in the 19th century as an outlet for the Arts and Crafts movement, the famous 'Tudor House' remains a leading stockist of young designers' clothes.

Around Covent Garden
Floral St (**B** C4) for Paul Smith, Nicole Farhi, Joseph, Maharishi; **Neal St** (**B** C3) for Carhartt, Birkenstock, and the Natural Shoe Store.

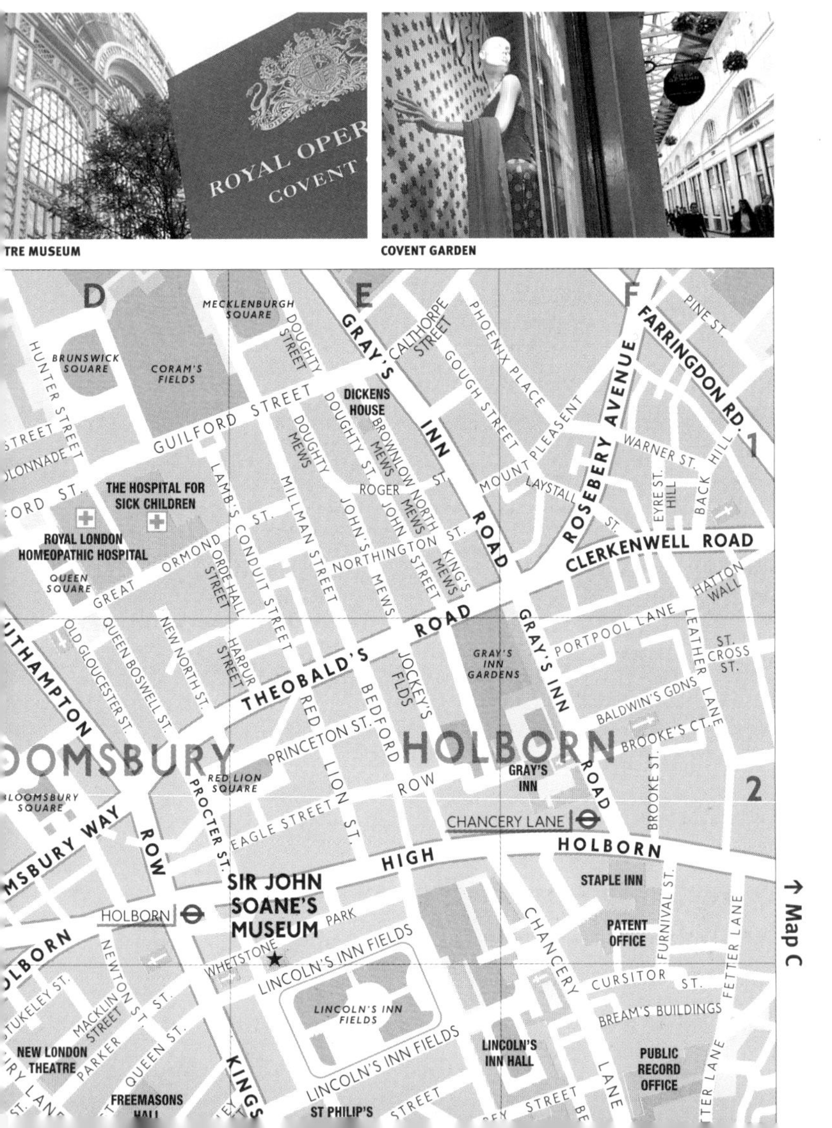

TRE MUSEUM

COVENT GARDEN

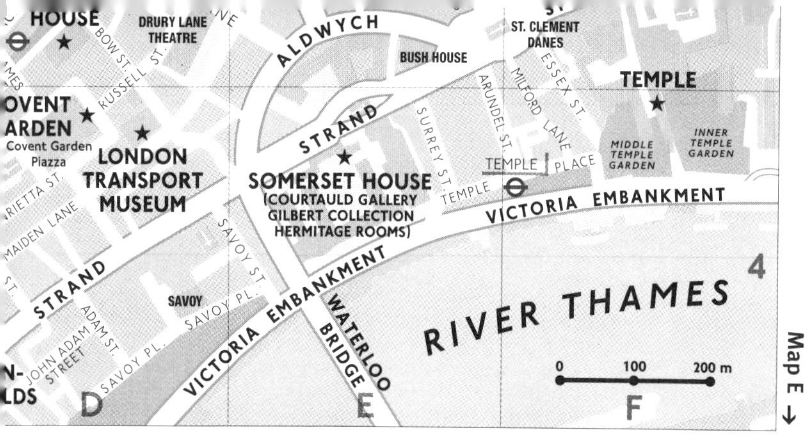

LE

ROYAL ACADEMY OF ARTS

ST MARTIN-IN-THE-FIELDS

splendidly restored
lassical building
es three museums:
ourtauld Gallery, with
npressive collection
pressionist and Post-
essionist paintings:
et, Monet, Gauguin,
arro, Renoir, Cézanne,
gliani, Van Gogh –
y all the major players
e movement are
sented. Also in the
ry are 32 works by
ns, a Botticelli *Trinity*
gouaches by Rouault;
**ilbert Collection of
rative Arts**, with some
pieces (gold and silver
, Italian *pietra dura*
ics, gold snuff boxes,
ait miniatures etc.);
and the **Hermitage Rooms**, whose rotating exhibitions display some of the finest objets d'art usually housed in the Hermitage Museum in St Petersburg – works amassed by one of the most prolific collectors of all time, Catherine the Great.

★ Temple (**B** F4)

This district, owned by the Knights Templar from 1185–1312, is like a small enclave within the city. Two of the four Law Schools took up residence here in the 17th century. On either side of Middle Temple Lane stretches a labyrinth of little streets, small courtyards and private gardens. This is also the site of the famous Middle Temple Hall, where Shakespeare's comedy *Twelfth Night* was premiered in 1600. Watch out for the pretty circular 12th-century church in the Inner Temple.

★ Royal Academy of Arts (**B** A4)

→ Burlington House, W1
Tel. 020 7300 8000
Daily 10am–6pm (10pm Fri); www.royalacademy.org.uk

The opening and complete refurbishment of the 'John Madejski' Fine Rooms, after more than 200 years, has allowed rare works by such artists as Gainsborough, Constable and Reynolds, to come out of storage. The Summer Exhibition still draws the crowds, as do the big-name shows which run throughout the year.

★ St Martin-in-the-Fields (**B** C4)

→ Trafalgar Square, WC2
Mon-Sat 8am–6.30pm (Sat 9am); Sun 8am–7.30pm

A church has stood here since the 13th century. This one, designed by James Gibb in 1726, transformed the architectural style of English religious buildings.

★ Theatre Museum (**B** D4)

→ Russell St, WC2
Tue-Sat 10am–6pm

Pictures, photos, models and accessories from the Elizabethan period (17th century) to the present day. Guided tours led by actors three times a day.

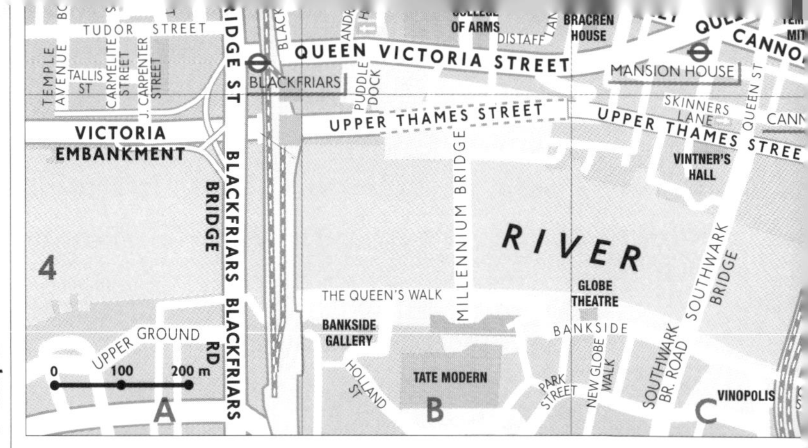

GUILDHALL

ST PAUL'S CATHEDRAL

★ **Tower of London** (**C** F4)
→ *Tower Hill, EC3*
Tel. 0870 756 6060 Tue-Sat 9–6pm; Sun-Mon 10am–6pm
William the Conqueror built this tower to control traffic on the Thames. The fortress was also used as a palace and a prison; John the Good, Anne Boleyn and Rudolph Hess were all imprisoned here. The Yeomen Warders, in Tudor costume, continue to guard the Crown Jewels and the Royal Insignia on display here, as well as the large collection of weapons.

★ **Monument** (**C** D4)
→ *Monument St, EC3*
Tel. 020 7626 2717
Daily 9.30am–5pm
Erected to commemorate the Great Fire (1666), this impressive 203-foot-tall column conceals a marble staircase in its base which leads to the top.

★ **St Stephen Walbrook** (**C** C3)
→ *39 Walbrook EC4*
Tue-Fri 11.30am–4pm
Christopher Wren's masterpiece, and one of his most elaborate and classical designs. The architect used this church to try out some of his ideas for St Paul's.

★ **Leadenhall Market** (**C** E3)
→ *Whittington Ave, EC3*
Mon-Fri 7am–4pm
Opulent Victorian market hall with cream and red metal arches surmounted by a glass dome at the intersection of its aisles. Close by, at 30 St Mary Axe, and visible from far away is Norman Foster's Swiss RE Tower (2004), a 40-story office building nicknamed 'the gherkin' by Londoners.

★ **St Paul's Cathedral** (**C** B3)
→ *St Paul's Churchyard, EC4*
Mon-Sat 8.30am–4pm; www.stpauls.co.uk
After the last war, the cathedral was left standing in the midst of the ruined City. Churchill had protected Wren's masterpiece, which became the symbol of the Londoners' indomitable spirit in the face of the Blitz. Its dome, which t[cut off] 26 years to reach completion in 1708, is t[cut off] largest in the world afte[cut off] that of St Peter's in Ro[cut off] and soars to a height o[cut off] 361 ft. The Golden Galle[cut off] its summit offers splen[cut off] views. The interior boa[cut off] some splendid 18th-ce[cut off] decorative treasures: wrought-iron choir gate[cut off] Tijou, frescos by Thorn[cut off] and choir stalls by Gib[cut off] The tombs of Wren and Nelson are in the crypt.

★ **Bank of England Museum** (**C** D3)
→ *Bartholomew Lane, EC*[cut off]
Mon-Fri 10am–5pm
Find out about the hist[cut off]

← Map E

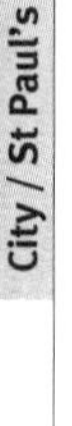

TOWER OF LONDON

MONUMENT

ST STEPHEN WALBROOK

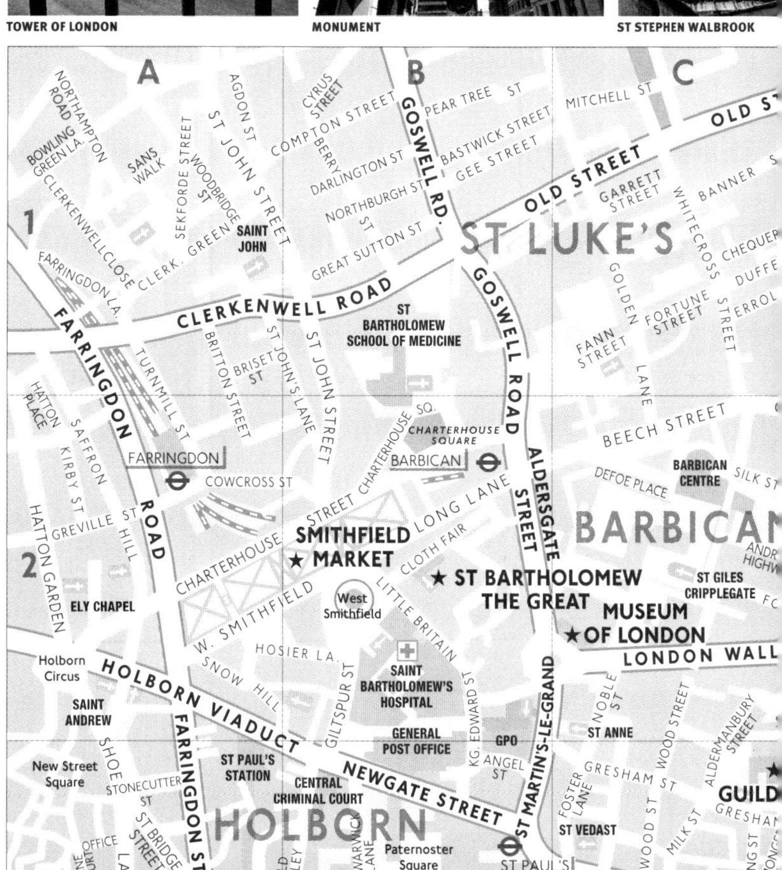

Men and women scurry around here during the week, making the area a hive of activity. By Saturday the City looks like a ghost town, and you have 48 hours to enjoy its deserted streets, suddenly ideal for a discovery tour. Relics of the past, spared by the Great Fire of 1666 and the air raids of World War Two, offer a glimpse into the historic heart of London. The maze of streets and alleys hold some surprises as dull, uninspiring granite and concrete 1960s office blocks stand alongside old pubs, historic churches and the innovative, graceful glass and steel constructions of the past few years. Although sparse, shopping is good and some of the best restaurants in London are found here.

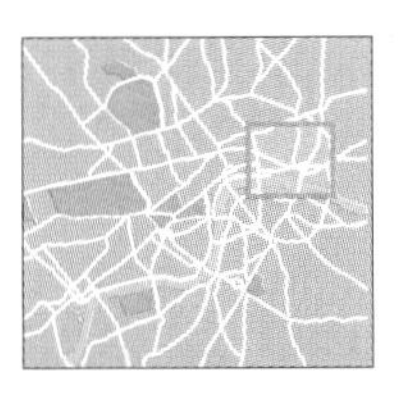

MOSHI MOSHI SUSHI

THE REAL GREEK SOUVLAKI

RESTAURANTS

Arkansas Café (**C** F2)
→ *Old Spitalfields Market, E1*
Tel. 020 7377 6999
Mon-Fri noon–2.30pm; Sun noon–4pm
A café at the center of the market, with a massive grill and pit barbecue, where you will eat some of the best steaks, burgers and grills in the city. £10.

The Place Below (**C** C3)
→ *Church of St Mary-Le-Bow, Cheapside, EC2*
Tel. 020 7329 0789
Mon-Fri 7.30am–3pm
Excellent vegetarian café. The Norman crypt makes for a beautiful, unusual setting. Eat in or take out.

Moshi Moshi Sushi (**C** E2)
→ *Liverpool St Station, upper level, EC2*
Mon-Fri 11.30am–9.30pm
This sushi bar, London's first *kaiten* (conveyor belt) when it opened in 1995, hangs above the platforms at Liverpool St Station. £15.

The Real Greek Souvlaki & Bar (**C** A1)
→ *140 St John St, EC1*
Tel. 020 7253 7234
Mon-Sat noon–11pm
Superior Greek 'street food', with lamb, pork or chicken kebabs (souvlakis) and mezedes whose ingredients vary with the seasons. Modern decor with high tables around a bustling, open kitchen. Very good list of Greek wines. Meze £3.50; souvlaki £5.75.

St John Bread and Wine (**C** F2)
→ *94-96 Commercial St , E1*
Tel. 020 7247 8924
Mon-Fri 9am–11pm; Sat-Sun 10am–11pm (10.30pm Sun)
The name St John became famous in the world of food when Fergus Henderson turned a canteen-like space on St John Street into a place of pilgrimage for anyone interested in contemporary eating – and in offals in particular. At this much informal place across from Spitalfields you are offered a simpler version of the same seasonal classics: ox heart & pickled walnut, pea and ham soup, crispy Welsh pig with dandelion & mustard. Delicious home-made bread and desserts. Busy, buzzing, friendly. £15.

The Peasant (**C** A1)
→ *240 St John St, EC1*
Tel. 020 7336 7726 Daily noon–11pm (10.300m Sun)
This atmospheric Victorian pub was, with The Eagle, one of the forerunners of the gastropub revolution Beautiful bar with round horseshoe counter at street level, and a gorgeous restaurant upstairs, with high ceilings, wide windows,

PEASANT

A. GOLD

OLD SPITALFIELDS MARKET

a fireplace in winter and a small terrace at the rear in summer. Surprising, delicious 'Asian-Med' food. Carte £20.

Club Gascon (**C** A2)
→ 57 West Smithfield, EC1
Tel. 020 7796 0600
Mon-Sat noon–2pm, 7–10pm
Toulouse-born chef Pascal Aussignac brings flair and an innovative sleight of hand to the grand food of southwest France – duck, cassoulet, but mainly foie gras – with tapas-size dishes and an amazing combination of flavors. Try the duck foie gras, frosted apple and pastis or, in season, the morels & broad beans casserole with refreshing rice crispies. Clean, clear decor; large bill. Five-course tasting menu and wines £65. Carte from £45. Two doors down is Le Comptoir Gascon, a wine bar and a cheaper alternative to the Club.

BARS, PUB, CLUB, CULTURAL CENTER

Royal Exchange Grand Cafe & Bar (**C** D3)
→ The Royal Exchange, Threadneedle St, EC3
Tel. 020 7618 2480
Mon-Fri 8am–10pm
The magnificent paved courtyard of the Royal Exchange, surrounded by a gallery of luxury boutiques, makes a great spot for a drink or light lunch. Breakfast and all-day menus available. Carte £15. At mezzanine level are two bars over-looking the courtyard and a restaurant, Sauterelle.

Loungelover (**C** F1)
→ 1 Whitby St, EC2
Tel. 020 7012 234
Tue-Sat 6pm–midnight
Owned by the same three friends who opened the no-less-hip restaurant Les Trois Garcons in the nearby Club Row. Glamorous eccentric decor (the boys were antique dealers) of sculpted stools, crystal chandeliers, and warm red walls. Long list of imaginative cocktails and a rather wealthy youthful clientele.

The Blackfriar (**C** B3)
→ 174 Queen Victoria St, EC4
Tel. 020 7236 5474
Mon-Sat 11am–11pm
An extremely popular and lovely pub with an elaborate Arts and Crafts-style decor depicting carved friars and young monks on the walls.

Fabric (**C** A2)
→ 77a Charterhouse St, EC1
Tel. 020 7336 8898
Fri 9.30pm–5am; Sat 10pm–7am; www.fabriclondon.com
The three rooms of this mythical club welcome the best DJs in the world and the most knowledgeable of dance music-loving crowds.

Barbican Centre (**C** C2)
→ Silk St, EC2
Tel. 020 7638 8891 Mon-Sat 9am–11pm; Sun noon–11pm; www.barbican.org.uk
Make the effort to visit this cavernous and austere maze of concrete (which, it is true, is more enjoyable when the terrace is bathed in sunshine). This is a major arts center and renowned concert hall for classical, jazz and world music, and contemporary dance. Great program of free music in the foyer.

SHOPPING

Old Spitalfields Market (**C** F2)
→ Brushfield St, E1
Mon-Fri 11am–4pm; Sun 9am–5pm; www.visitspitalfields.com
Sadly the number of stalls at this much-loved old covered market, built in 1682 (and a survivor of assaults over the years, including the Blitz), has been recently reduced to make way for trendy new office buildings and more lucrative retail premises. During the week (but mostly Sun): knickknacks, new-age products, hip and retro clothes by young talented designers, accessories; organic produce on Fri and Sun. Other interesting stores around the market.

A. Gold (**C** F2)
→ 42 Brushfield St, E1
Tel. 020 7247 2487
Daily 11am–8pm (6pm Sun)
British produce, made to traditional methods, sold in a shop which looks like a cottage: cakes, jams, gingerbread, bacon pies, cheeses, pickles etc.

Lesley Craze (**C** A1)
→ 33-35a Clerkenwell Green, EC1 Tel. 020 7608 0393
Mon-Sat 10am–5.30pm
Small shop-gallery dedicated to the work of young designers. Beautiful modern fabrics, decorative pieces and items of jewelry.

MAGMA (**C** A1)
→ 117-119 Clerkenwell Rd, EC1 Tel. 020 7242 9503
Mon-Sat 10am–7pm; www.magmabooks.com
A great shop with a vast choice of books on subjects such as computer design, typography and photography. It also sells fun T-shirts. Annex on West St (**B** C3).

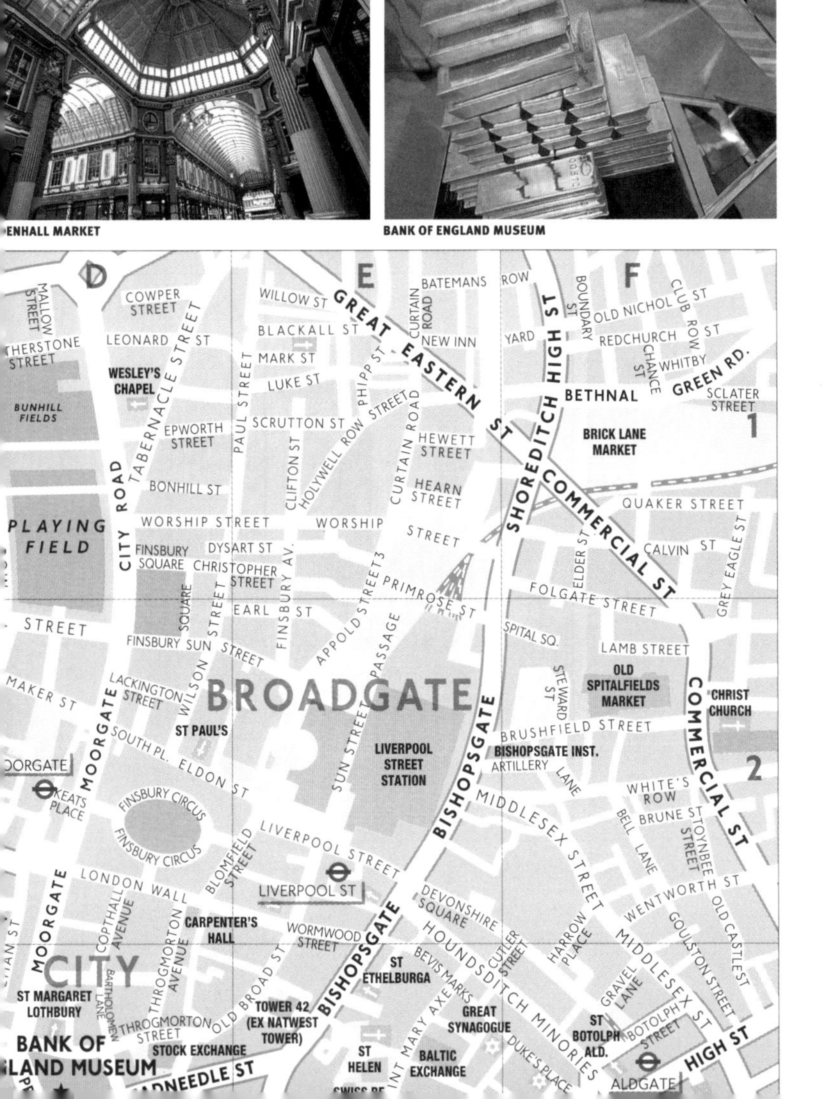

ENHALL MARKET

BANK OF ENGLAND MUSEUM

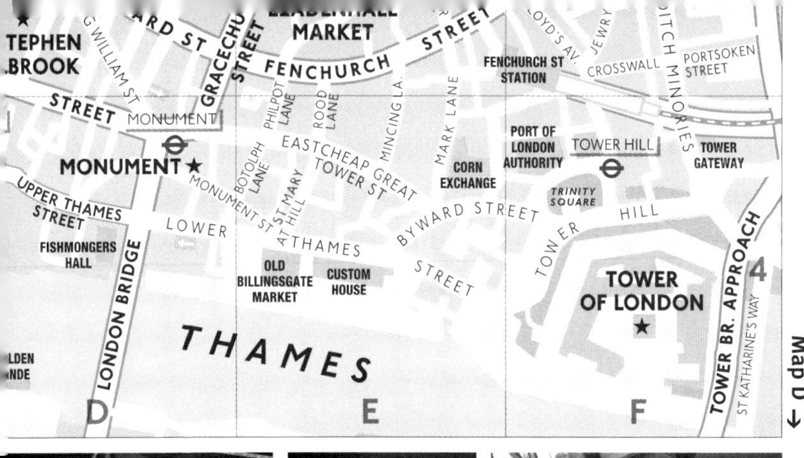

G WILLIAM ST	G RACECHU STREET	LEADENHALL MARKET

STEPHEN BROOK

ARD ST

FENCHURCH STREET

LLOYD'S AV. JEWRY ITCH STREET

PORTSOKEN STREET

STREET

MONUMENT

PHILPOT LANE

ROOD LANE

MINCING LA.

MARK LANE

FENCHURCH ST STATION

CROSSWALL MINORIES

MONUMENT ★

BOTOLPH LANE

ST MARY AT HILL

EASTCHEAP GREAT TOWER ST

CORN EXCHANGE

PORT OF LONDON AUTHORITY

TOWER HILL

TOWER GATEWAY

UPPER THAMES STREET

MONUMENT ST HILL

LOWER

A THAMES

BYWARD STREET

TRINITY SQUARE

TOWER HILL

FISHMONGERS HALL

STREET

OLD BILLINGSGATE MARKET

CUSTOM HOUSE

STREET

TOWER OF LONDON ★

TOWER BR. APPROACH

LDEN NDE

LONDON BRIDGE

T H A M E S

ST KATHARINE'S WAY

4

D

E

F

EUM OF LONDON

ST BARTHOLOMEW THE GREAT

SMITHFIELD MARKET

day-to-day running e 'Old Lady of adneedle Street', the erful Bank of England, h stores the nation's in its coffers.

uildhall (C C2) resham St, EC2 20 7332 3700 ry: Mon-Sat 10am–5pm; noon–4pm heart of the City's icipal power beats nd this remarkable -century façade, h reflects a fusion of ic, Greek and Indian ences. Passing under ierceron ribbed vault, r the great stone hall × 49 ft), site of official monies. The walls are

decorated with the arms of all the guilds that have elected the Lord Mayor since 1319. The names of all the mayors are inscribed on the stained-glass windows. Don't miss the art gallery, which displays around 4,000 works illustrating the history of London.

★ **Museum of London (C** C2)
→ *London Wall, EC2 Tel. 020 7600 0807 Daily 10am (noon Sun)–5.50pm; www.museumoflondon.org.uk*
A fascinating museum devoted to the story of London and the life of its people, from prehistory to the present day. It offers animated reconstructions

(including the Great Fire of 1666), models, everyday items, relics and costumes.

★ **St Bartholomew the Great (C** B2)
→ *Church House Clothfair, EC1 Tue-Fri 8.30am–5pm (4pm Nov-Jan); Sat 10.30am–1pm; Sun 8.30am–1pm, 2.30–8pm*
The oldest church in London (12th century) has had a checkered past. After Henry VIII's ban on religious orders in the 16th century, the north transept was used as a forge, the crypt as a cellar, the Lady Chapel as lodgings then as a printing house, and the cloister as a stable. The church was restored and again used for worship in the 19th century.

The massive pillars of the ambulatory are one of the few examples of Norman architecture in London.

★ **Smithfield Market (C** B2)
→ *Charterhouse St, EC1 Mon-Fri 3am–noon (come before 7.30am)*
Monumental Victorian buildings designed by Sir Horace Jones in 1866–8 on a square which, in the Middle Ages, used to stage public executions. From 1868 they housed the city's main meat market. Today, the beautiful cast-iron arches, red-brick walls and glass-roofed halls of Smithfield are threatened by land developers.

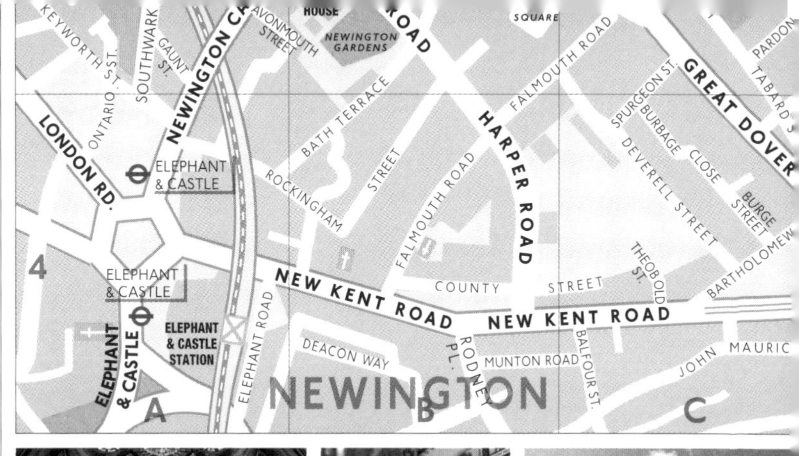

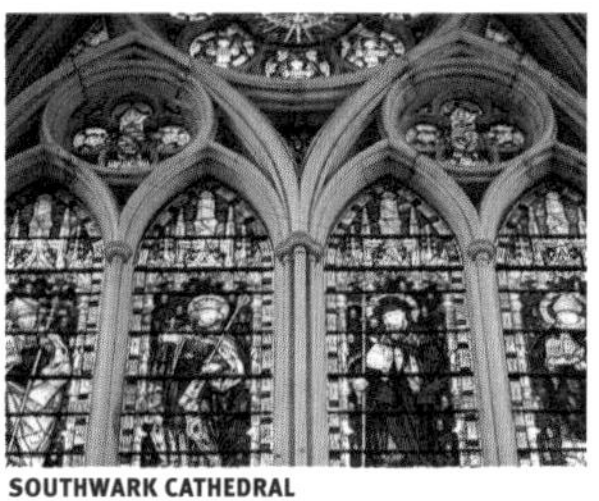
SOUTHWARK CATHEDRAL

VINOPOLIS

SHAKESPEARE'S GLOBE EXHIBITION

★ **Tower Bridge** (**D** E1)
→ *Tel. 020 7403 3761*
Daily 10am–6.30pm (9.30am–6pm in Oct-March)
As much a symbol of London as Big Ben, the distinctive silhouette of Tower Bridge evokes the Victorian era when England was a powerful seafaring nation. River traffic was extremely heavy at that time and the movable bridges were raised to allow ships to pass through. The two neo-Gothic towers conceal the complex hydraulic lifting machinery used to raise the two 1,000-ton bascules. A museum recounts the history of the bridge.

★ **HMS *Belfast*** (**D** D1)
→ *Morgan's Lane, SE1*
Tel. 020 7940 6300
Daily 10am–6pm (5pm Nov-Feb)
Experience the life of a sailor on board a warship. This one was in service from 1938 to the end of the Korean War in 1953.

★ **Design Museum** (**D** F2)
→ *28 Shad Thames, SE1*
Tel. 020 7940 8790
Daily 10am–5.45pm; www.designmuseum.org
The brainchild of design guru Sir Terence Conran, this museum is devoted to the study of design for mass production. Examples of everyday items such as chairs, telephones, radios, cameras and washing machines are testament to the esthetic revolutions heralded by the industrial era. The first floor hosts temporary exhibitions on technological advances and design trends.

★ **Southwark Cathedral** (**D** C1)
→ *Montague Close, SE1*
Daily 9am–6pm
One of the few vestiges of the district's medieval past, William Shakespeare's brother Edmund is buried here. The church has been remodeled on many occasions but the current building retains the choir and the ambulatory of Gothic church (1273). T triforium was inspired t the cathedrals of Chart and Reims in France. Th is a fine recumbent sta of a knight made of car oak (13th century).

★ **Hay's Wharf** (**D** D1
In the 19th century, merchant ships were lo and unloaded along th bustling quays of the Thames. The two impre red brick and light stor buildings were once us as warehouses for stor butter and spices. They connected by a passag with a glazed barrel va supported by a slende

↑ Map C

DESIGN MUSEUM

TOWER BRIDGE

HMS *BELFAST*

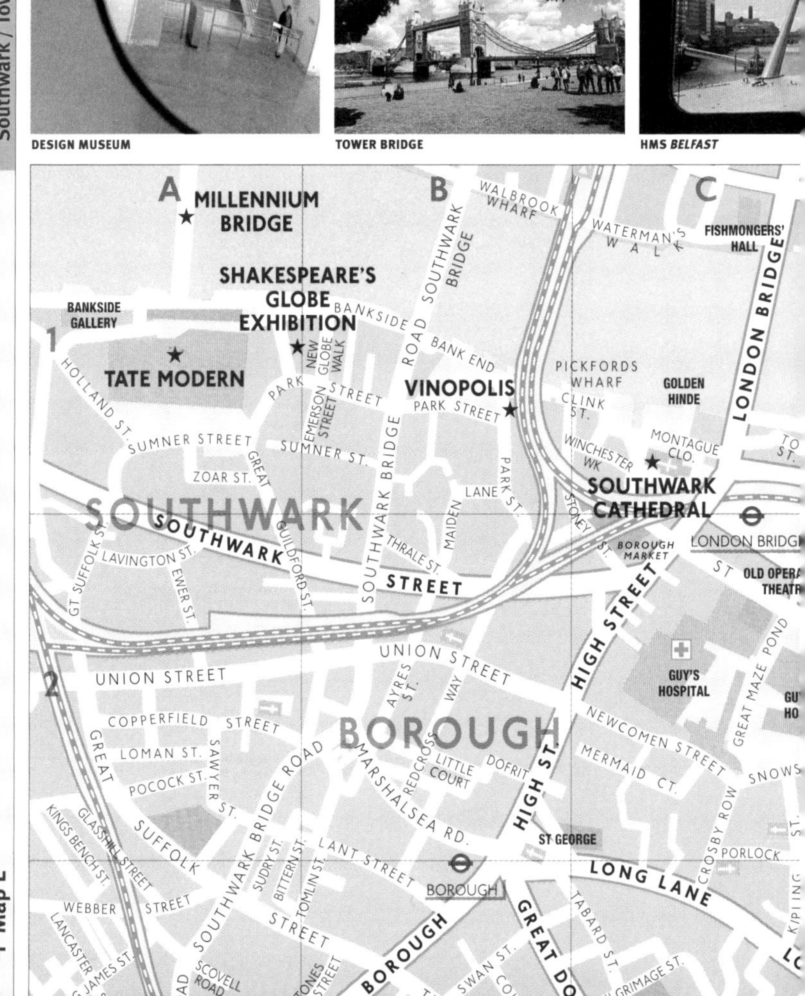

↑ Map E

Southwark had always been London's poor relation and, with its brothels, taverns and theaters, a dumping ground for unwanted people and pastimes. The docks ushered in a period of prosperity but the district suffered anew when they were closed in 1950. Various new projects and restoration programs followed after the Design Museum opened in 1989, culminating in the inauguration of the Tate Modern in May 2000. The two are linked by Queen's Walk, a very pleasant riverside path. Wealthier people have taken up residence in the area, but further south are still some of the capital's least fashionable districts.

À la carte prices are given per person for a starter and a main course. Drinks and service are not included.

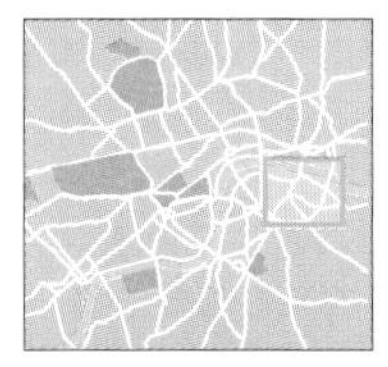

TAS PIDE

FISH!

RESTAURANTS

M. Manze (**D** E3)
→ *87 Tower Bridge Rd, SE1*
Tel. 020 7407 2985
Tue-Thu 10.30am–2pm; Fri -Sat 10am–2.15pm; Mon 11am–4pm;
Pie, eels and mash is a hearty meal exemplifying London's culinary traditions. Take out or eat in the 100-year-old canteen-like restaurant. The place is as much an attraction as the food. From £3.

El Vergel (**D** B2)
→ *8 Lant St, SE1*
Tel. 020 7357 0057
Mon-Fri 8am–3pm
A colorful Latin-American deli, five minutes from Borough subway station. Sandwiches, Mexican salads and first-class service. Specialty: Torta Mexicana sandwich with chicken, beans and guacamole. £5–10.

Tas Pide (**D** B1)
→ *20-22 New Globe Walk, SE1. Tel. 020 7928 3300*
Daily noon–11.30pm (10.30pm Sun)
The entrance to this small restaurant is facing the Globe Theater. Interesting, tasty Anatolian (Turkish) cuisine and *pide*, a sort of pizza dough in the shape of a boat, baked on site and garnished with mouthwatering ingredients – the *pide* with grilled sardines wrapped in vine leaves, onions, olives and lemon zest is delicious. Small, light, very pleasant room. Menus from £8.75.

Bermondsey Kitchen (**D** D3)
→ *194 Bermondsey St, SE1*
Tel. 020 7407 5719
Mon-Fri noon–3pm, 6.30–10.30pm; Sat 9.30am–3.30pm, 6.30–10.30pm; Sun 9.30am–3.30pm
A relaxed, friendly bar & gastropub a few doors from Delfina below. The kitchen is in full view of the diners, with a huge charcoal grill as its centerpiece. Ingredients come extra-fresh from the nearby Borough market or from Essex. Short, seasonal menu, and excellent brunch (until 2pm) at the weekends. Tapas (from £1.95) if you want to snack. Cocktails from £5. Carte £16–20.

Delfina Studio Café (**D** D2)
→ *50 Berdmondsey, SE1*
Tel. 020 7357 0244
Mon-Fri noon–3pm (also 7–10pm Fri); café: Mon-Fri 8am–noon, 3–5pm
Delfina is an interesting place, having once been a chocolate factory, then

VINOPOLIS WINE WHARF

BOROUGH MARKET

NEAL'S YARD DAIRY

the canteen of the artists in residence. The light, airy café has blossomed, and the Studio is today better known for the bright, modern, delicious food it serves than for the changing exhibitions next door. New menu every two weeks. Carte £20. Across the road is London's first fashion and textile museum (closed Mon).

Fish! (**D** C2)
→ *Cathedral St, Borough Market, SE1*
Tel. 020 7407 3803
Mon-Thu 11.30am–11pm, Fri-Sun noon–11pm
With its steel and glass structure, Fish! looks very much like an aquarium. The delicious dishes depend on the daily deliveries: squid, fresh cod, skate, swordfish – you name it, grilled or steamed. Carte £24.

Lightship (**D** F1)
→ *5a St Katharine's Way, E1*
Tel. 020 7480 6116
Tue-Sat noon–3pm, 6–10pm (closed Sat lunch)
Beautifully refurbished and docked by Tower Bridge, this is the oldest surviving lighsthip in the world, built in 1877. British Scandinavian cuisine with an emphasis on fish and seafood. Book ahead for dinner. Menus £26–31.

CAFÉS

Maria's Market Café (**D** C2)
→ *Borough Market, SE1*
Tel. 020 7407 5048 Mon-Sat 5.45am–4pm (2.30pm Sat)
If your heart is set on a traditional English breakfast, this café, deep in the heart of Borough, is one of the best. Not exactly fat-free but there are lighter alternatives.

Design Museum Café (**D** F2)
→ *28 Shad Thames, SE1*
Tel. 020 7940 8785
Daily 10am–5.30pm
A very pleasant small museum café, whose floor-to-ceiling glass windows give onto the river. Above is Terence Conran's smart Blueprint restaurant, with even better views of the Thames (*open Mon-Sat for lunch & dinner, Sun for lunch only; tel 020 7378 7031*).

BAR, PUB, CLUB

Vinopolis Wine Wharf (**D** B1)
→ *Stoney St, SE1*
Tel. 020 7940 8335
Mon-Sat noon–11.30pm; www.winewharf.co.uk
A huge wine bar under the high brick arches of an old bridge, with a list of over 300 vintages sold by the glass. There is a more intimate tapas bar tucked away in a recess.

The Anchor (**D** B1)
→ *34 Park St, SE1*
Tel. 020 7407 1577
Mon-Sat 11am–midnight; Sun noon–11pm
Built in 1770, this old pub has preserved its maze of small dark rooms. In summer the large terrace with wooden tables is perfect for enjoying a drink in the sunshine. Docked just outside the pub is the 16th-century *Golden Hinde*.

Ministry of Sound (**D** A3)
→ *103 Gaunt St, SE1*
Tel. 020 7378 6528 Fri 11pm–5am; Sat 11pm–7am; www.ministryofsound.com
More than a nightclub, the Ministry is a brand and a legend with an exceptional sound system. Three dance floors play techno, garage and house music.

SHOPPING

The Christmas Shop (**D** D1)
→ *Hay's Galleria, 55A Tooley St, SE1*
Tel. 020 7378 1998
Mon-Fri 8.30am–6pm; Sat-Sun 10.30am–5.30pm
A shop devoted to beautiful and original Christmas decorations.

Borough Market (**D** C2)
→ *London Bridge, SE1*
Thu 11am–5pm; Fri noon–6pm; Sat 9am–4pm
The oldest food market in London (1756), and one that chefs seem to like best. Under the railway lines, behind Southwark Cathedral, stalls and small stores sell mostly organic produce – spices (try the smoked paprika sold in the Brindisi store), meat, fish, cheese, oils, bread, cakes (those from Konditor & Cook are delicious) and more.

Neal's Yard Dairy (**D** B2)
→ *Borough Market, 6 Park St, SE1*
Tel. 020 7500 7653 Mon-Fri 9am–6pm; Sat 8am–4pm
Shelves from floor to ceiling are piled with maturing wheels of farmhouse cheeses.

Bermondsey Market (**D** D3)
→ *Bermondsey St, SE1*
Fri 4am–2pm
Each Friday antique stalls spread through the streets of this district, which is full of second-hand furniture stores. The market is frequented by many dealers – proof that there are bargains to be had if you're an early riser.

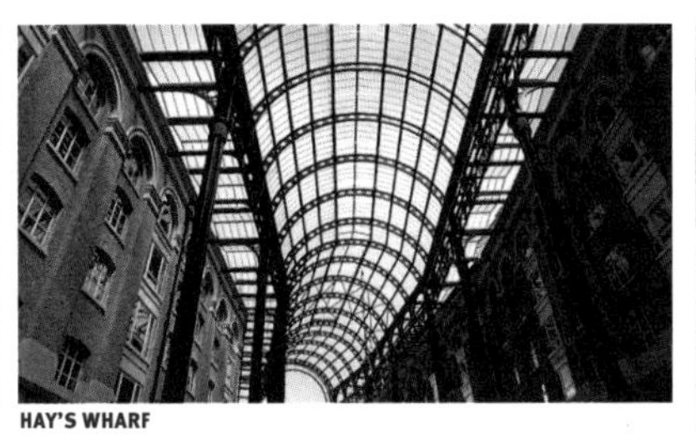

HAY'S WHARF

LONDON DUNGEON

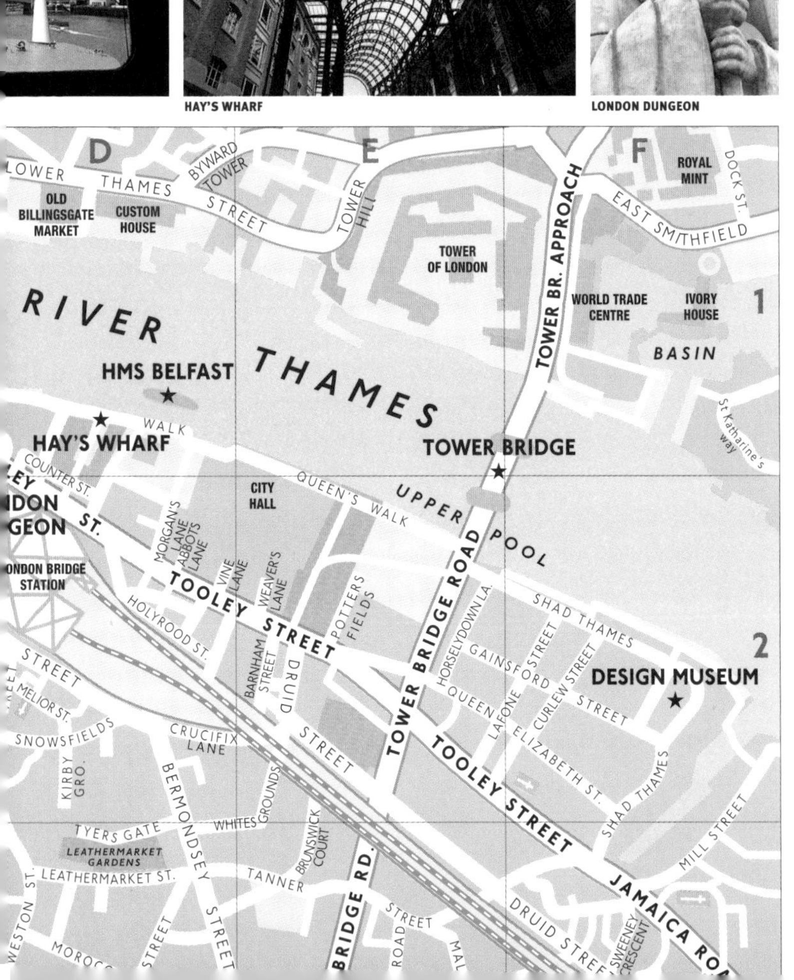

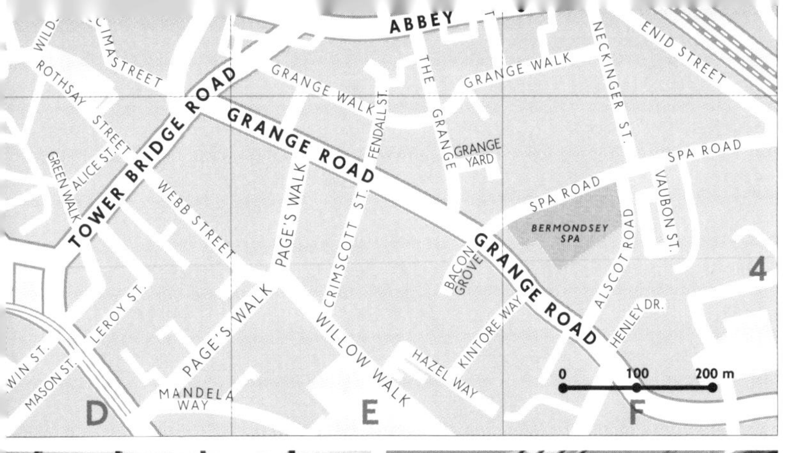

MODERN

MILLENNIUM BRIDGE

-l framework which -s to a height of 98 ft. -vatively renovated by -g, Brown & Partners -e 1980s, the Hay's -eria now houses cafés, -aurants and stores.

-ondon Dungeon (**D** C2)
-8–34 Tooley St, SE1
-020 7403 7221
- 10am–5.30pm (times call ahead)
figures, dark cells, -my corridors: enjoy -ste of the macabre -nst a background of -country's key historical -nts. No children under 10.

-inopolis (**D** B1)
-Bank End, SE1
-870 444 4777
Daily noon–6pm (9pm Mon, Fri-Sat); last entry two hours before; www.vinopolis.co.uk
A museum/exhibition looking at wine-producing around the world. Tastings are organized too, with a guide (for those over 18).

★ Shakespeare's Globe Exhibition (**D** B1)
→ New Globe Walk, SE1
Tel. 020 7902 1500
Daily 10am–5pm (9am–noon in May-Sep); www.shakespeares-globe.org
A museum charting the epic reconstruction of the Globe, Shakespeare's theater. Ten years in the making, it was built close to the original site, using 17th-century materials and techniques.

★ Tate Modern (**D** A1)
→ Bankside, SE1
Tel. 020 7887 8000 Daily 10am–6pm (10pm Fri-Sat); www.tate.org.uk
The splendid achievement of architects Herzog and Meuron has finally given London an international museum of modern art. Stripped of its boilers and turbines, the 1947 power station now has 100,000 square feet of galleries. Arranged thematically, these house the whole of the Tate's collection of modern art and temporary exhibitions. The Turbine Hall soars to a height of 115 ft and functions as a reception area. Extremely well-stocked bookstore. Restaurant on the top floor affords great views over St Paul's and the Thames.

★ Millennium Bridge (**D** A1)
→ Across from Tate Modern
The first bridge to be built in London for over a century opened in May 2000, it closed two days later due to wobbling. Re-opened two years later the steel foot bridge, designed by Norman Foster and Partners in collaboration with sculptor Anthony Caro, now safely links the south bank with St Paul's.

BFI SOUTHBANK

ROYAL FESTIVAL HALL

★ **Blackfriars Bridge** (**E** D1)
Beneath this colorful bridge with its surbased steel arches, a series of frescos illustrate the history of the surrounding area and the role played by the River Thames. The present structure dates from 1869, but a bridge has stood on this spot since 1769. At that time it was the third to straddle the river: until 1738 London Bridge was the only bridge connecting the two banks.

★ **BFI Southbank** (**E** B2)
→ *South Bank SE1*
Tel. 020 7928 3232 Daily 11am–11pm; www.bfi.org.uk
Formerly known as the National Film Theatre, this is the temple of cinema in London, with three screens for movies, retrospectives and talks, and a library that holds the world's largest collection of information on film and television. Major events are organized such as the London Film Festival, which screens international movies in the fall. The BFI IMAX cinema, which has the UK's largest movie screen, is close by (**E** C3).

★ **Gabriel's Wharf** (**E** C2)
→ *56 Upper Ground, SE1*
Craft stores and boutiques, children's play area and café terraces. The little square and the few surrounding square yards would have ended up in the hands of a real estate developer, like the rest of the district, but for the tireless battle waged by the non-profit making Coin Street Community Builders.

★ **National Theatre** (**E** B2)
→ *South Bank, SE1*
Tel. 020 7452 3400 Mon-Sat 9.30am–11pm. Guided tours Mon-Sat: 10.15am, 12.15pm, 5.15pm (the latter not on Sat); (75 mins); www.nt-online.org
Although this may look like a fortress the National, as it is simply known, is one of the most acclaimed theaters in the city. Designed by Denys Lasdun in 1975, this concrete building has three auditoriums which stag everything from avant- g plays to spectacular big name musicals. Guidec tours take you backstag for a fascinating look at the stage machinery (th tour starts in the main which mounts exhibitic of contemporary art).

★ **South Bank Centre** (**E** B2)
→ *Belvedere Rd, SE1*
www.sbc.org.uk
The controversy (its criti felt that the chilly gray concrete shouldn't have been left without adorn that surrounded this ar center after its construc in 1951 has now more o died down. A recent ma

BLACKFRIARS BRIDGE

GABRIEL'S WHARF

A
B
1
2
3
4
COVENT GARDEN
LONG AC.
FLORAL ST
KING ST
ST PAUL'S
BEDFORD STREET
HENRIETTA ST
COVENT GARDEN
LONDON TRANSPORT MUSEUM
DRURY LANE THEATRE
WELLINGTON ST
RUSSELL ST
CATHERINE ST
EXETER ST
SOUTHAMPTON ST
MAIDEN LANE
CHANDOS PL.
WILLIAM IV STREET
STRAND
SAVOY CHAPEL
SAVOY ST
SAVOY PL.
ADAM ST
JOHN ADAM ST
VILLIERS ST
CHARING CROSS
CRAVEN STREET
EMBANKMENT
ALDWYCH
LANCASTER PL.
BUSH HOUSE
ST MARY'S LE-STRAND
SURREY ST
TEM
COURTAULD GALLERY GILBERT COLLECTION
EMBANKMENT
VICTORIA
WATERLOO BRIDGE
NA
T
BFI SOUTHBANK
WATER
QUEEN'S W.
QUEEN ELIZABETH HALL
HAYWARD GALLERY
SOUTH BANK CENTRE
ROYAL FESTIVAL HALL
ROAD
NORTHUMBERLAND AVENUE
WHITEHALL PLACE
HUNGERFORD BRIDGE
OLD WAR OFFICE
HORSE GUARDS AV.
BANQUETING HOUSE
VICTORIA EMBANKMENT
THAMES
QUEEN'S WALK
JUBILEE GARDENS
BELVEDERE
SHELL CENTRE
WAT
LONDON EYE
ROAD
RICHMOND TERRACE
DALÍ UNIVERSE
CHICHELEY STREET
RD
SOU
BAN
COUNTY HALL
LONDON AQUARIUM
YORK
BELVEDERE
WESTMINSTER
HALL OF FAME
ADDINGTON STREET
BRIDGE ST
WESTMINSTER BRIDGE
BIG BEN
FLORENCE NIGHTINGALE MUSEUM
HOUSES OF PARLIAMENT
ROAD
KMENT
R
Old

There are few surviving vestiges of this area's past; the swamps were drained centuries ago and the last war decimated the factories and workshops which, in the 19th century, had transformed these villages into an important industrial center. The land on the south bank was subsequently cleared of rubble to build cultural facilities capable of rivaling those on the north bank. The South Bank Arts Centre, completed in the 1960s, was the first building in this complex and many others have been built since. Queen's Walk now extends alongside the river, affording fine views of the buildings across the water.

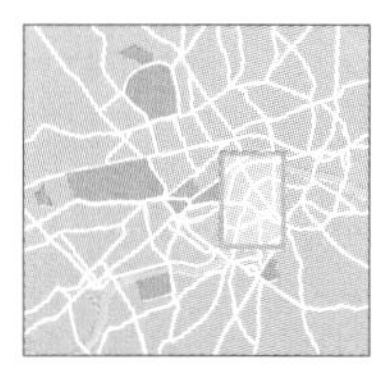

MESON DON FELIPE

LIVEBAIT

RESTAURANTS

Meson Don Felipe (**E** D3)
→ *53 The Cut, SE1*
Tel. 020 7928 3237
Mon-Sat noon–midnight
First-class tapas bar serving the usual small-sized portions of Spanish delicacies – light, tasty and made with the freshest ingredients. The place is packed and noisy in the evening, with flamenco guitarists playing most nights. Very good wines at very good value. Carte £15.

Laughing Gravy (**E** D3)
→ *154 Blackfriars Rd, SE1*
Tel. 020 7721 7055 Mon-Fri noon–11pm; Sat 7–11pm
Forget the bland exterior, this is a warm, homely, quiet bar-gastropub, where many locals hang out because the food is spot on and reasonably priced. Try the incredibly tender bison or rib-eye steak, the crab or what they call all-day 'light bites', which are in fact very generous snacks. Belgian beers and Breton cider. Carte £18.

Anchor & Hope (**E** D3)
→ *36 The Cut, SE1*
Tel. 020 7928 9898
Mon 6–10.30pm; Tue-Sat noon–2.30pm, 6–10.30pm
The gastropub of the south bank, co-founded by two chefs who learned their skills at St John (see **C**) among other places. Adventurous, changing menu of a rather rich cuisine: snail and bacon risotto, ox cheeks, lamb sweetbreads, pigeon and semolina gnocchi. Simple decor of wooden tables and chairs. No bookings taken so you may have to wait in the bar area, especially at the weekend. Carte £20–25.

Livebait (**E** D3)
→ *43 The Cut, SE1*
Tel. 020 7928 7211
Mon-Sat noon–11pm; Sun 12.30–9pm
White and green tiled seafood restaurant whose fresh fish and friendly ambience have been a winning formula since it opened in 1998. Dishes are of the utmost simplicity along with some clever combinations, such as oven-baked halibut with couscous and sweet potato tagine. Carte £22. Pre-theater menu £19.50.

The People's Palace (**E** B2)
→ *Royal Festival Hall, South Bank, SE1*
Tel. 020 7928 9999
Daily noon–3pm, 5.30–11pm
Get a seat by the window

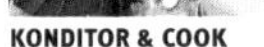

KONDITOR & COOK

OXO TOWER

GANESHA

in this high-ceilinged restaurant with views over the Thames. The food is modern, British-European and the place is especially popular for Sunday lunch, and, of course, before or after concerts. Pre-concert menu £16.50. Carte £25.

Baltic (**E** D3)
→ *74 Blackfriars Rd, SE1*
Tel. 020 7928 1111
Mon-Sat noon–3pm, 6–11pm; Sun noon–11pm
It has a long, seductive bar, a vast dining room with a glass roof supported by oak beams, and a modernist, gray decor that can seem rather cold – somewhat less so once you've tried some of the 40 types of vodka available. Fantastic Polish and modern Eastern-European food is on offer: marinated herrings with cucumber, potato and dill salad; paprika chicken with spiced bean salad and garlic yogurt. The desserts are also very good. Carte £25. Live jazz every Sun evening at 7pm.

BARS, PUBS

OXO Tower Bar (**E** C2)
→ *OXO Tower, Eighth floor Wharf Barge House St, SE1*
Tel. 020 7803 3888 Mon-Sat 11am–midnight (11pm Mon-Wed); Sun noon–10pm
This floor of the OXO tower offers exhilarating views of the Thames and north bank, especially in the evening when the sky is clear. Have a drink at the bar amidst a mix of City suits and romantic couples, then go down five floors (to the second) to the newly-opened Japanese yakitori restaurant Bincho.

Cubana (**E** C3)
→ *48 Lower Marsh, SE1*
Tel. 020 7928 8778
Mon-Fri noon–midnight (3am-Fri); Sat 5pm–3am
This bar will brighten your spirits in any weather. Drinks and music reflect the Latin American theme. Religious trinkets, brightly colored chairs, portraits of Che and photos of Cuba adorn the walls. The two bars serve cocktails, wine, bottled beer and snacks. Salsa, Wed 10.30pm–12.30am; Thu 11pm–1am; Fri-Sat 11pm–3am.

Namco Play Station (**E** B3)
→ *Riverside Building, County Hall, SE1*
Tel. 020 7967 1066
Daily 10am–midnight
A modern paradise for devotees of video games, simulators and amusement arcades. Try your hand at the latest game or race around in the fastest bumper cars in Europe. Also has billiard tables, a bowling alley, a bar and giant screens.

SHOPPING

Konditor & Cook (**E** C3)
→ *22 Cornwall Rd, SE1*
Tel. 020 7261 0456
Mon-Fri 7.30am–6.30pm; Sat 8.30am–2.30pm
If you are feeling peckish or looking for a last-minute gift, this tiny deli behind Waterloo Station is irresistible – and constantly voted one of London's best by chefs and restaurateurs. The cakes are mostly baked on the premises and all the delicacies are made with the finest ingredients.

What the Butler Wore (**E** C4)
→ *131 Lower Marsh, SE1*
Tel. 020 7261 1353
Mon-Sat 11am–6pm
A small, secondhand clothes store for lovers of 1960s and 1970s garb. Everything is in excellent condition and, given the number of revivals, usually look bang up-to-date. Dresses from £30. No credit cards.

Gramex (**E** C4)
→ *25 Lower Marsh, SE1*
Tel. 020 7401 3830
Tue-Sat 11am–7pm
This legendary haunt for fans of classical music boasts a wide range of secondhand vinyl discs and CDs. The staff are helpful and well informed and music lovers often carry on their conversation in the large armchairs at the rear of the store.

OXO Tower Design Shops (**E** C2)
→ *OXO Tower Wharf, Barge House St, SE1*
Tel. 020 7401 2255
Tue-Sun 11am–6pm
The restored Art Deco Oxo Tower Wharf now houses a complex of shops-cum-workshops belonging to independent designers, some of whom sell their designs here exclusively. Hand-woven silk, jewelry, children's clothes, porcelain and small pieces of furniture.

Ganesha (**E** C2)
→ *3 Gabriel's Wharf, SE1*
Tel. 020 7928 3444
Tue-Fri 11.30am–6pm; (11am Mon); Sat-Sun noon–6pm; www.ganesha.co.uk
Colorful store selling fair-trade products such as cushions, bags and spreads from India, Nepal and elsewhere.

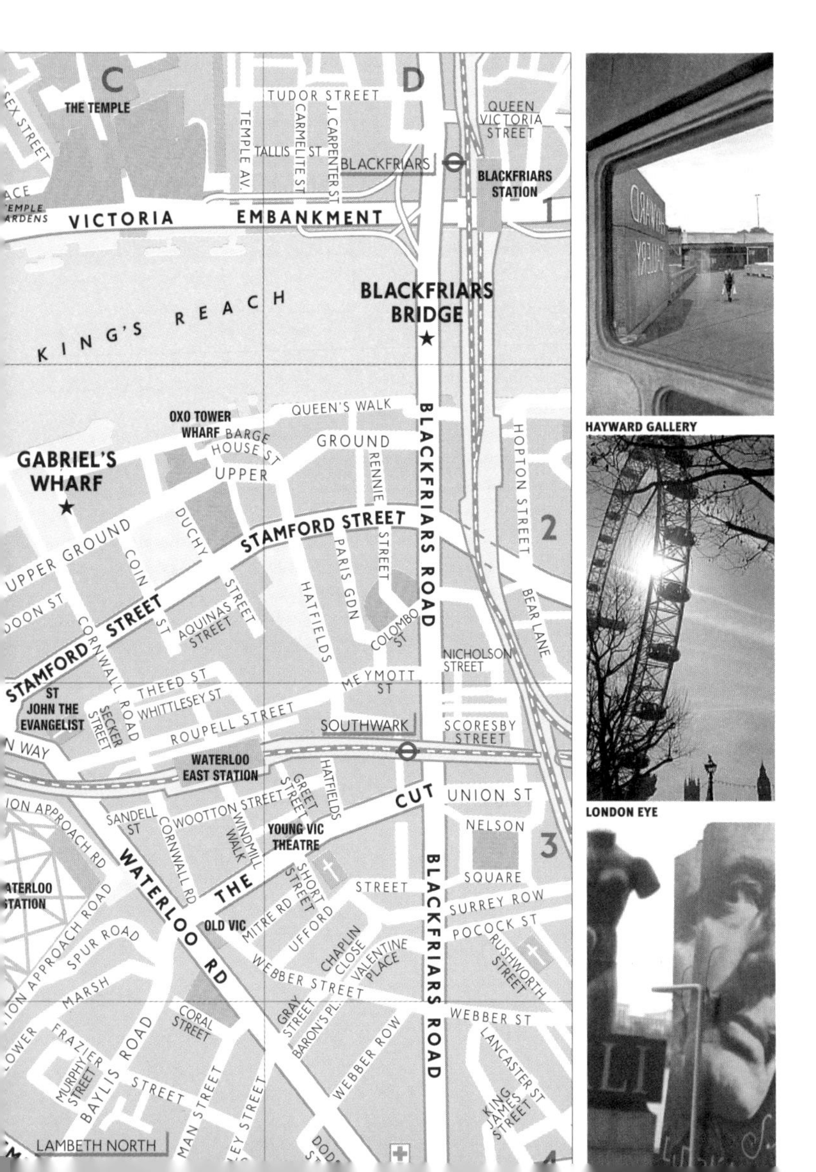

HAYWARD GALLERY

LONDON EYE

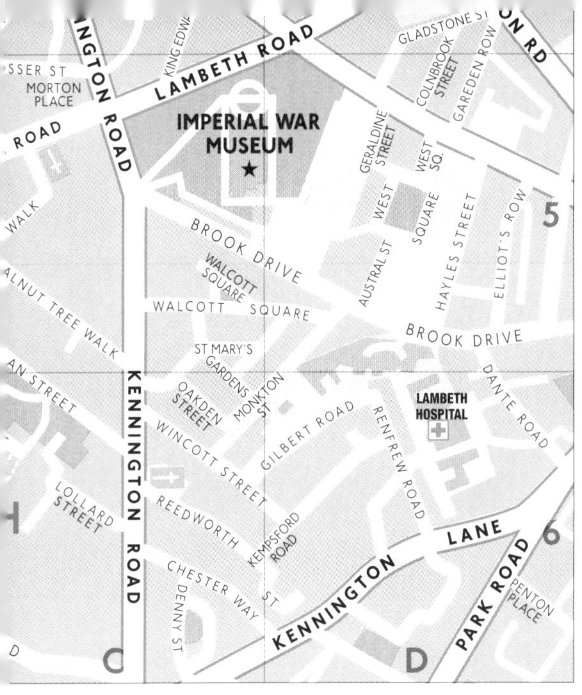

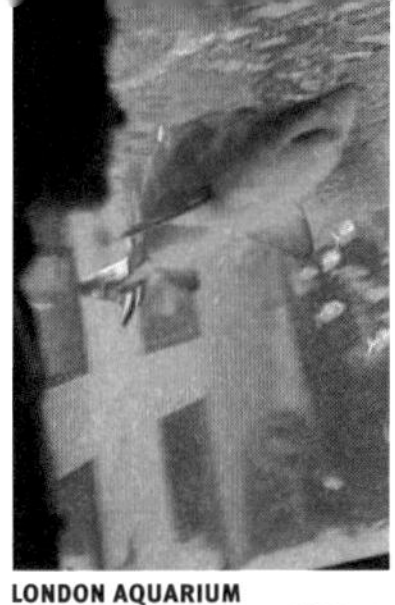

LONDON AQUARIUM

IMPERIAL WAR MUSEUM

ram of renovation has
ɔ the opening of many
urants and cafés along
mbankment to make
outh Bank more
oming. Visitors,
ever, never ceased
ing to the concert hall,
vated by its vast
or spaces flooded
light. It's worth a visit
g the day to listen to
e lunchtime concert, or
nply relax and enjoy
nk looking at the river.

l Festival Hall
t concert hall with
ptional acoustics and
perb program of jazz,
ical, rock and pop.

ell Room
aller hall for recitals and chamber music, again with excellent acoustics.

Queen Elizabeth Hall
Dance and classical music.

Hayward Gallery (E B2)
→ *Daily 10am–6pm (8pm Fri-Sat)*
Major painting, sculpture and photography exhibitions are shown in this stark concrete gallery, to which a glass pavilion designed by New York-based artist Dan Graham, was added in 2003.

★ London Eye (E B3)
→ *South Bank, SE1*
Tel. 0870 500 0600
Daily 10am–9pm (8pm Oct-May); booking recommended
Take a 40-minute trip on the tallest wheel in the world. From a height of 443 ft you enjoy (in good weather!) spectacular views over London. On a clear day you can see for 25 miles.

★ County Hall (E B3)
→ *Riverside Building, County Hall, SE1*

London's Aquarium
→ *Tel. 020 7967 8000*
Daily 10am–6pm
Stroke the rays, watch the sharks being fed and discover fresh-water and salt-water fish from all over the world.

Dalí Universe
→ *Tel. 020 7620 2720*
Daily 10am–6.30pm
A museum opened in 2004 for the centenary of Dalí's birth, and entirely devoted to him. With 500 of his works (drawings, objects, sculptures) arranged thematically within three sections (Sensuality and Femininity, Religion and Mythology and Dreams and Fantasy), this makes for a fascinating journey into the mind of the Surrealist artist.

★ Imperial War Museum (E C5)
→ *Lambeth Rd, SE1*
Tel. 020 7416 5000
Daily 10am–6pm
An unrivalled collection of war memorabilia. In the basement, special attention is paid to the two World Wars; the upper floors are given over to a very moving study of the Holocaust.

SHERLOCK HOLMES MUSEUM

WALLACE COLLECTION

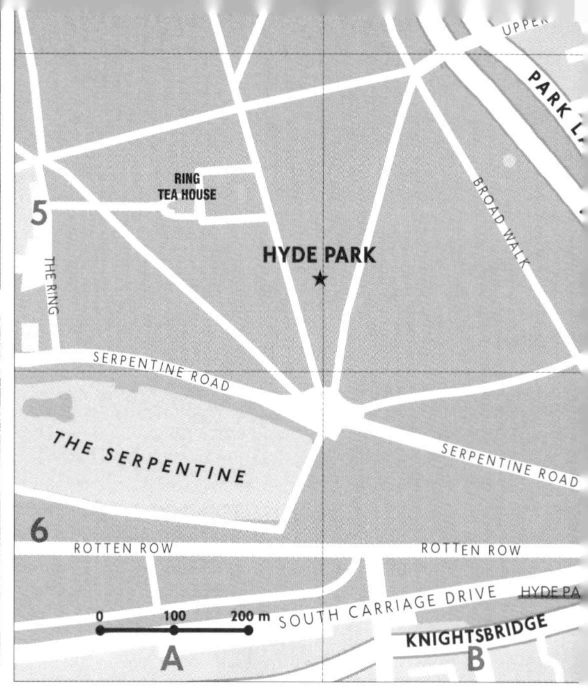

← Map G

★ **Regent's Park** (**F** C1)
→ *Daily 5am–sunset*
In 1811, John Nash, already a famous architect, obtained the backing of the future King George IV to realize his dream of creating an idealized garden city on farmland once belonging to the Duke of Portland. Nash wanted terraces around the sides of the park with high porticos, tall stuccoed façades and massive colonnades. Inside he envisaged grand mansions while more modest houses clustered together in romantic villages were to be situated around the perimeter. Only part of the dream was ever realized, but this superb green space has many other attractions including tennis courts, cricket pitches, a zoo, the magnificent Queen Mary Rose Garden and the Open Air Theatre which stages *A Midsummer's Night's* Dream every summer.

★ **Madame Tussaud's** (**F** B1)
→ *Marylebone Rd, NW1*
Tel. 0870 999 0293
Mon-Fri 9.30am–5.30pm; Sat-Sun 9am–6pm
This famous waxworks is still the third most popular attraction in London. The Chamber of Horrors in the basement never fails to chill the heart. Next door is the former planetarium which now shows an animated movie, *The Wonderful World of Stars*, by the same team who produced *Wallace and Gromit*.

★ **Handel House Museum** (**F** D4)
→ *25 Brook St, W1*
Tel. 020 7495 1685
Tue-Sun 10am–6pm (8pm Thu); Sun noon–6pm
The house where Handel (1685–1759) spent the end of his life. Exhibits include manuscripts, paintings and scores. Concerts.

★ **Wallace Collection** (**F** C3)
→ *Manchester Square, W1*
Tel. 020 7935 0687 Mon-Sat 10am–5pm; Sun noon–5pm; www.wallacecollection.org
The 4th Marquess of Hertford (1800–70) wa dandy, an eccentric an well-informed collecto was passionately inter in painting (Hals, Fragc Rembrandt, Velasquez Poussin, Watteau), fur (Riesener and Boulle), objets d'art, and Easte and Western weaponry armor. His illegitimate Richard Wallace, conti to swell this priceless collection which was bequeathed to the Sta 1897 on condition that works were never to le the museum. The hous refurbished and enlarg 2000 for the collection 100th birthday.

REGENT'S PARK

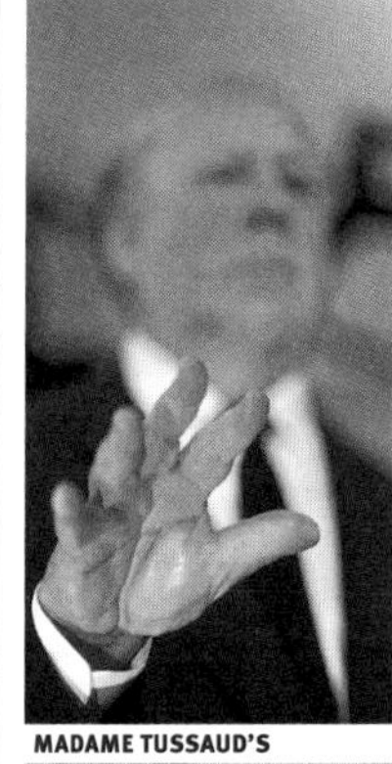
MADAME TUSSAUD'S

Mayfair has the reputation of being the classiest district in London. Although Vivienne Westwood, the subversive creator of the 1970s' punk look, opened a shop here, the prestigious hotels and luxury stores on New and Old Bond streets are more in keeping with the district's upmarket image. Marylebone, further north, is more lively, particularly around Marylebone High Street, with its striking Georgian façades and astonishing array of clothes shops and good restaurants. Around Regent's Park there are many neoclassical marvels including John Nash's magnificent Cumberland Terrace, with its blue and white pediment in the east.

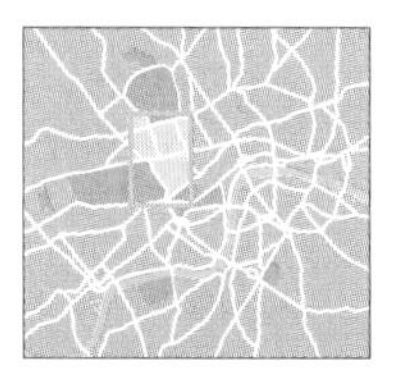

THE PROVIDORES

WIGMORE HALL

RESTAURANTS

Carluccio's Café (**F** C3)
→ *St Christopher's Place, off Oxford St, W1*
Tel. 020 7935 5927
Mon-Fri 8am–11pm; Sat-Sun 9am–10.30pm
One of the many deli-restaurants of Italian chef Antonio Carluccio. St Christopher's Place itself is worth a visit, as it is a surprising haven of peace behind the hustle of Oxford Street. Eat in or take out. Carte £10.

The Providores and Tapa Room (**F** C2)
→ *109 Marylebone High St, W1 Tel. 020 7935 7175*
Mon-Fri 9am–11pm; Sat-Sun 10am–10.30pm
The Providores is a restaurant on the first floor (book ahead) and a Tapa Room, which is a combination of wine-bar, tapas bar and breakfast bar (no advance booking) on the ground floor. Excellent cooking on both floors, a fusion of Eastern and Western flavors. Carte £50. Tapa Room £20.

Ping Pong (**F** C3)
→ *29a James St, W1*
Mon-Sat noon–11pm; no booking policy; seven other branches in London
'Yum cha' means to drink tea and 'dim sum' to 'touch the heart'. For the latter no better place than Ping Pong, where the freshly made, fragrant steamed dumplings – try the king prawns and bamboo shoots or snow crab, prawns and scallops in carrot tortellini pastry – should get your attention. Black, soothing decor. From £2.99 per portion (plan at least four per person). Interesting and reasonably-priced cocktails (try the kumquat mojito or vodka with lemongrass, lime and lychee).

Orrery (**F** C1)
→ *55 Marylebone High St, W1 Tel. 020 7616 8000*
Daily noon–2.30pm, 6.30–11pm (10.30pm Sun-Wed)
Terence Conran has created here a deliciously suave dining area out of what is, really, a long thin room and, ten years after its opening, his only Michelin-starred restaurant is still a gem. The service is impeccable, the wine list very expensive but remarkable and the food glorious. Very good value, three-course, set lunch menu: £24. Carte £40–55. Book ahead.

Gordon Ramsay at Claridge's (**F** C4)
→ *49 Brook St, W1*
Tel. 020 7499 0099 Mon-Sat

FRIDGES

NEW BOND STREET

CHARBONNEL & WALKER

noon–3pm, 5.45–11pm; Sun noon–2.45pm, 6–10.30pm
Three-Michelin-starred Gordon Ramsay is undoubtedly one of the best and most passionate chefs in Britain today. His Claridge's restaurant is an exceptional Art Deco setting for what should be a memorable meal. Excellent value set lunch or pre-theater three-course menu (£30). Book well in advance.

CAFÉ, TEAROOMS

Café 88 (**F** C3)
→ 88 Wigmore St
Tel. 020 7224 2188
Mon-Sat 7am–7pm
Simple café with seemingly nothing extra to offer that the many surrounding eateries cannot, but it always comes across as an oasis of calm after the crowds and busy-ness of Oxford St and Selfridges. Quiches, salads, sandwiches etc. Lovely staff.

The Conservatory (**F** C6)
→ Lanesborough Hotel, Hyde Park Corner, SW1
Tel. 020 7259 5599
Daily 3.30–6pm (4pm Sun)
Be more British than the British and sample the delights of afternoon tea in one of London's most stylish hotels. Delicate sandwiches and scones with jams and clotted cream are served in a tiered winter garden.

De Gustibus (**F** B2)
→ 53 Blandford St, W1
(also 53 Carter Lane, C B3)
Tel. 020 7486 6608
Mon-Fri 6.30am–4pm
Artisan bakers are getting rare, so it is a genuine pleasure to sit in this traditional bakery lined with wrought-iron shelves and pots of jam. Fantastic breads and patisseries, obviously.

BARS, PUBS, CONCERT HALLS

Tudor Rose (**F** B2)
→ 44 Blandford St, W1
Tel. 020 7935 5963
Mon-Sat 11am–11pm
Traditional Scottish pub with a white half-timbered façade, dark wood paneling and an open fire. It serves first-class meals which can be eaten in the small dining room or on the terrace in summer.

Wigmore Hall (**F** C3)
→ 36 Wigmore St, W1
Tel. 020 7935 2141
www.wigmore-hall.org.uk
Built in 1901 by the Bechstein Piano firm, this building is a gem of a recital hall with fantastic acoustics. Chamber music and songs.

SHOPPING

Geo F. Trumper (**F** D5)
→ 9 Curzon St, W1
Tel. 020 7499 1850 Mon-Fri 9am–5.30pm; Sat 9am–1pm
Shaving brushes in all shapes and sizes, fine razors, colognes and aftershaves: the last word in men's beauty products. Act the dandy and have the perfect shave, manicure (except Sat) or haircut at one of the most famous gentleman's stores in the city.

Selfridges (**F** C3)
→ 400 Oxford St, W1
Tel. 0870 837 7377
Mon-Sat 9.30am–8pm (9pm Thu); Sun noon–6pm
Huge department store stocking most fashion labels, with something to suit everyone's purse. Well known for its menswear collections, postcard shop and food hall (although the latter doesn't compare with Harrods').

Whistles (**F** C3)
→ 12 St Christopher's Place, W1 Tel. 020 7487 4484
Mon-Sat 10am–7pm; Sun noon–5pm
Beautifully feminine clothes made with brightly colored, sometimes embroidered, fabrics.

South Molton St (**F** C3)
Pedestrian, store-lined street. Browns: all fashion labels and their permanent sale shop, Labels for Less, at no. 50.
Kurt Geiger, Pied à Terre, Dune, Jones for women's shoes. Poste: shoes for men. Butler and Wilson for bags and accessories.

Old and New Bond streets (**F** D3-4)
The epitome of elegant shopping. Among the many shops are:
Smythson of Bond Street for leatherbound stationery.
Ventilo, Miu Miu, Jimmy Choo, MaxMara, Bulgari, Prada, Armani, Alexander McQueen for men's and women's fashion.
Georg Jensen, Boucheron, Cartier, Asprey, Tiffany for the most beautiful jewelry in the world; and Fenwicks, Bond Street's smart department store.

Charbonnel & Walker (**F** D4)
→ 28 Old Bond St
Mon-Sat 10am–6pm
High-quality chocolates, some flavored with mint, lavender, raspberry, rose or violet, made in the time-honored English tradition. The dark chocolate eggs sold at Easter are divine.

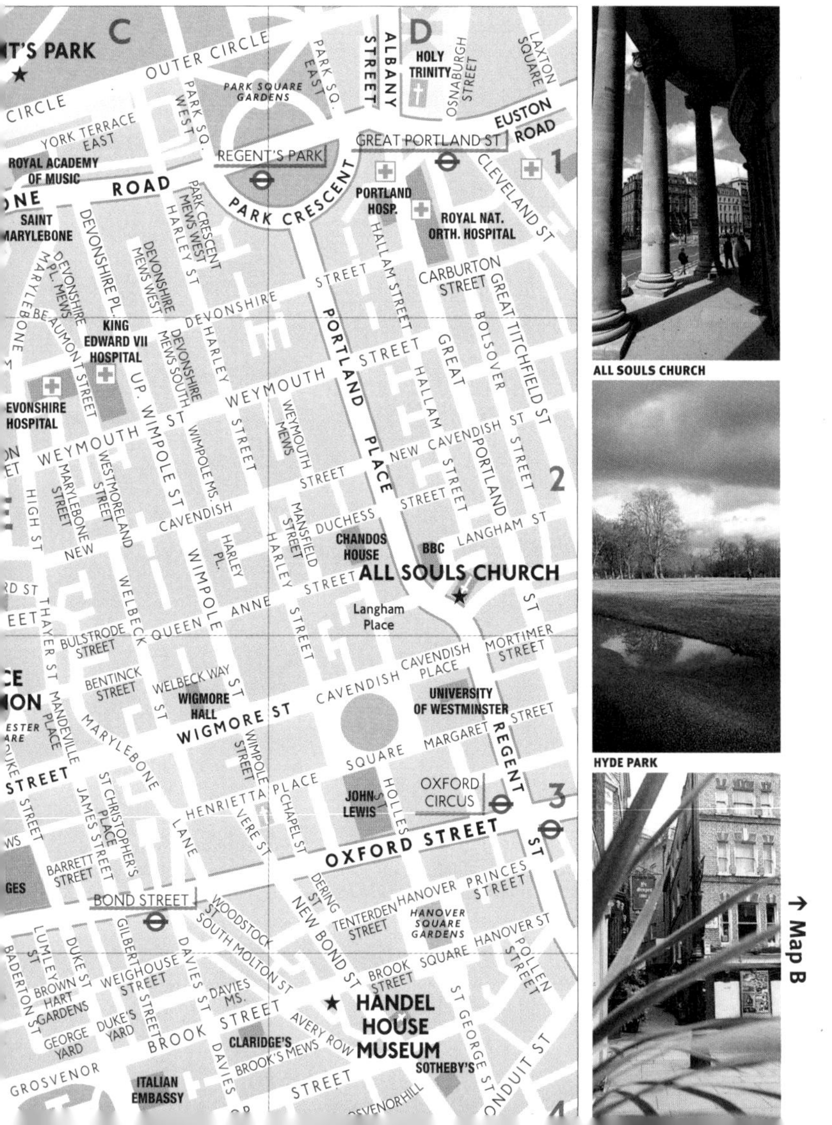

ALL SOULS CHURCH

HYDE PARK

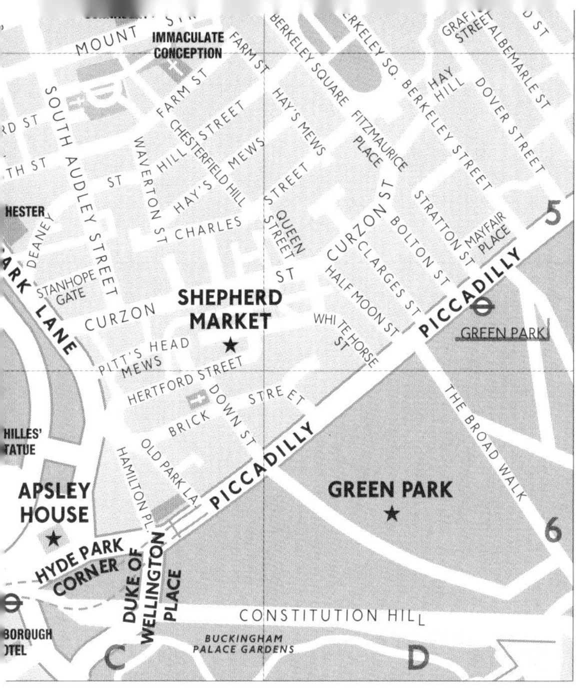

ASPLEY HOUSE

GREEN PARK

Map A →

herlock Holmes seum (**F** B1)
21b Baker St, NW1
020 7935 8866
9.30am–6pm
are shown round the er-sleuth's Victorian rtments by his house- per, Mrs Hudson.

ll Souls Church (**F** D2)
ngham Place, W1
-Fri, Sun 10am–6pm
n it was completed 324, this church, the one built by John Nash is still standing, was ned by some critics wedding cake.

yde Park (**F** A5)
aily 5am–midnight
don's most popular park e an immense green lung at the city's center. Bathers, boats and swans ply up and down the Serpentine, where a midnight swim is held every year at Christmas. Riders parade along Rotten Row and the lawns are inviting for a siesta. Since 1872, would-be orators have aired their opinions at Speaker's Corner; anyone can stand on a makeshift platform and have their say here as they attempt to rally passersby to their cause.

★ **Shepherd Market** (**F** C5)
→ *Between Curzon St and Piccadilly*
West of crowded Piccadilly, this haven of peace calls to mind a little hamlet threaded with pedestrian streets and scattered with appealing paved courtyards. This used to be the center of the May Fairs (cereals and cattle) from which the entire area derived its name. Good variety of cafés and pubs.

★ **Apsley House** (**F** C6)
→ *Number One, London Hyde Park Corner, W1*
Tel. 020 7499 5676 Tue-Sun 10am–5pm (4pm Oct-March)
'Number One, London', as the house is also known, was given to Wellington as a reward for his victory over Napoleon at the Battle of Waterloo (1815). He was also given many paintings and precious objects by influential figures, a collection which he enhanced with various spoils of war. Paintings by great masters (Velasquez, Goya, Rubens etc.); sculpture (Canova's Naked Napoleon); silver and gold plate; and priceless porcelain. Unfortunately the museum does not have a pair of the Iron Duke's famous Wellington boots.

★ **Green Park** (**F** D6)
→ *Daily 5am–midnight*
Extensive lawns, shady plane and lime trees, cast-iron benches and old gas lamps. Originally a leper's burial ground, no flowers are planted as a mark of respect for the dead below.

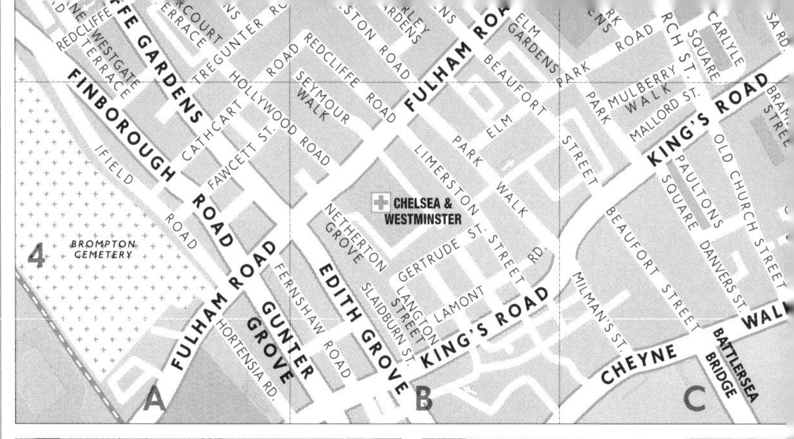

BELGRAVE SQUARE

SAATCHI GALLERY

★ Christie's South Kensington (G B2)
→ *85 Old Brompton Rd, SW7*
Tel. 020 7930 6074
Mon-Fri 9am–5pm (7.30pm Mon); Sat-Sun 10am–4pm
Visit the illustrious dealer where objets d'art and other items are auctioned.

★ Natural History Museum (G B2)
→ *Cromwell Rd, SW7*
Tel. 020 7942 5000
Daily 10am–5.50pm; www.nhm.ac.uk
Even the façade of the museum, one of Europe's largest, is swarming with plants and animals. There are 78 million specimens kept here, but only a small part of the collection is exhibited, charting the history and diversity of life on Earth, from dinosaurs to earthquakes. This is a fascinating museum but so big it is a good idea to plan your visit with the help of the website or a guide at the museum.

★ Science Museum (G C2)
→ *Exhibition Rd, SW7*
Tel. 0870 870 4771
Daily 10am–6pm; www.sciencemuseum.org.uk
A museum at the cutting edge of scientific progress. Interactive attractions and simulations abound on the four floors, an amazing showcase for the latest in scientific development (cloning, the most recent mission to Mars, advances in genetic engineering). The old rooms focus on the leading inventions of the industrial era, including a V2 missile, the Apollo 10 command module or George Stephenson's *Rocket*.

★ Victoria & Albert Museum (G C2)
→ *Cromwell Rd, SW7*
Tel. 020 7942 2000
Daily 10am–5.45pm (10pm Fri); www.vam.ac.uk
The 'V&A' houses one of the world's great collections of decorative arts. Exhibition galleries stretch for over 6 miles, and 4 million pieces are on display in 146 rooms. There is a vast variety of European and Asiatic objects including Raph tapestry cartoons, India fabrics and Korean cera The section on Indian a unmatched outside Ind The museum also hous collections of sculpture photography and painti In 2000, after an ambit reorganisation program new 'British Galleries' w opened. They tell the st British design from the of Henry VIII to that of Queen Victoria. More th 3,000 objects are on sh some in their original surroundings by way of restored period room

★ Brompton Oratory (G C2)
→ *Brompton Rd, SW7*

CHRISTIE'S

NATURAL HISTORY MUSEUM

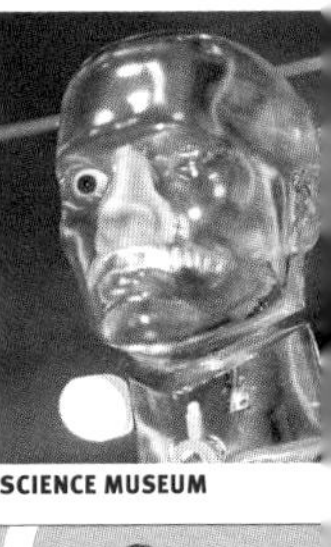

SCIENCE MUSEUM

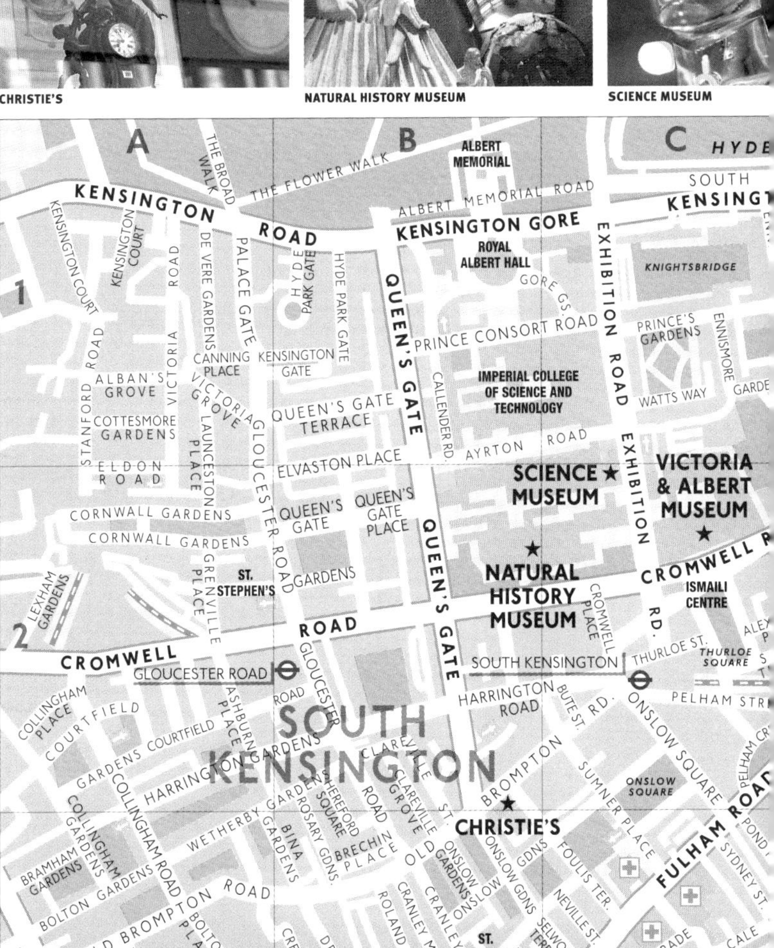

Take a stroll through an area that exudes stylish elegance: from South Kensington's world-class museums and on to Knightsbridge, epicenter of luxury shopping with Harrods and Sloane Street, the showcase of haute couture. Further east, embassies and aristocratic residences hide behind the impressive façades of Belgravia, a world away from the lively village atmosphere of Chelsea. Here you can give free rein to extravagant impulses in the boutiques and inviting cafés or enjoy a more economical stroll past antique stores and along the pretty streets which, before World War Two, were home to penniless and bohemian artists.

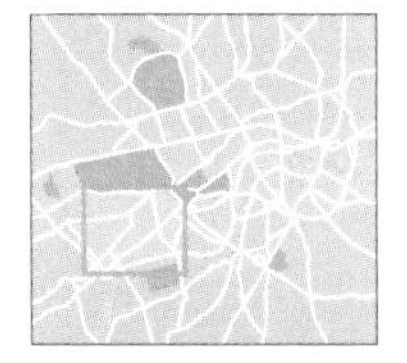

THE BUILDER'S ARMS

BIBENDUM

RESTAURANTS

Jenny Lo's Tea House (**G** F2)
→ *14 Eccleston St, SW1*
Tel. 020 7259 0399
Mon-Fri noon–3pm, 6–10pm; Sat 6–10pm
A wide variety of noodle and rice dishes in cheerful surroundings. Try the rice with eggplant in a Tuban soy sauce or seafood noodles with black beans. Carte £13.

The Builder's Arms (**G** D3)
→ *13 Britten St, SW3*
Tel. 020 7349 9040 Mon-Sat noon–2.30pm, 7–10pm; Sun noon–4pm, 6–9pm
Opposite the gardens of St Luke's, this modern pub, lit via light shafts, has been given a bold face-lift and is now more of a gastropub. The countless corners and comfortable sofas give the place a very easygoing, rather intimate feel. Good Mediterranean-inspired cuisine and a decent selection of wine by the glass. Carte £15.

Cambio de Tercio (**G** A3)
→ *163 Old Brompton Rd, SW5 Tel. 020 7244 8970*
Daily noon–2.30pm (3pm Sat-Sun), 7–11pm
The outspread capes of matadors adorn the walls of this warm and tempting restaurant. Mouthwatering choice of tapas for starters (clams, squid, Galician octopus) and perfect paellas. Excellent wine list. Reservation advisable at the weekend. Carte £22.

Bibendum (**G** C3)
→ *Michelin House, 81 Fulham Rd, SW3 Tel. 020 7581 5817*
Mon-Fri noon–2.30pm, 7–11pm; Sat-Sun noon–3pm, 7–11pm (10pm Sun)
An old tire factory very prettily converted, with amazing Art Deco stained-glass windows. The ground-floor oyster bar is cheaper than the restaurant but the latter's prices reflect Matthew Harris' excellent cuisine. Carte £30. Set menu £24.

Chutney Mary (**G** C3)
→ *535 King's Rd, SW10*
Tel. 020 7351 3113 Mon-Sat 12.30–2.30pm, 7–11pm; Sun 12.30–3pm, 7–10pm
Same owners as Masala Zone (see **B**), same high-quality ingredients but a more elaborate menu. The result is superb and the food plays on the full range of Indian flavors with subtlety. Carte £38.

Zafferano (**G** E1)
→ *15 Lowndes St, SW1*
Tel. 020 7235 5800
Daily noon–2.30pm (3pm Sun), 7–10.30pm

TMENT 195

HARRODS

CHELSEA FARMERS' MARKET

Very stylish, very accomplished genuine Italian fare by celebrated chef Giorgio Locatelli – tuna and scallops carpaccio with fennel and mint, wild seabass with artichokes puree and, of course, some of the best pasta dishes you'll have ever tasted. The two- to four- course set menus (£25.50–£45) are very good value. Book well in advance.

ICE CREAM PARLOR, BARS, PUB

Oddono's (**G** C2)
→ *14 Bute St, SW7*
Tel. 020 7052 0732
Daily 11am–11pm
The best Italian ice creams in London – some even say the best outside Italy. Homemade, with an unbeatable range of flavors to choose from.

Apartment 195 (**G** D3)
→ *195 King's Rd, SW3*
Tel. 020 7351 5195
Mon-Sat 5–11pm
Ring the bell of this discreet Chelsea address and walk upstairs to the 'apartment', a glamorous recreation of a New York-style loft with views over King's Road, and where Chelsea's smart set lounges around sipping cocktails. Efficient service, charming staff and a good list of drinks. DJs on Fri and Sat.

Bistrot 190 (**G** B1)
→ *190 Queen's Gate, Gore Hotel, SW7*
Tel. 020 7584 6601
Daily 7am–11pm
The walls of this hotel bar are covered with red wood paneling and the colonial-style decor, like the sofas, encourage you to sit back and take it easy. Ideal for a drink after a visit to one of the many museums nearby.

Cactus Blue (**G** C3)
→ *86 Fulham Rd, SW3*
Tel. 020 7823 7858
Mon-Sat 5pm–midnight;
Sun noon–11pm
A paradise for fans of tequila. There are dozens on the menu, imported from all over the world.

The Anglesea Arms (**G** C3)
→ *15 Selwood Terrace SW7*
Tel. 020 7373 7960
Mon-Sat 11am–11pm;
Sun noon–10.30pm
A very English gastro-pub with glass and wood partitions, creating small private areas, flowery Laura Ashley-type wallpaper and a terrace in spring and summer. The food isn't too expensive, and is consistently good.

CONCERT HALL

Royal Albert Hall (**G** B1)
→ *Kensington Gore, SW7*
Tel. 020 7838 3110
Tours (45 mins): Fri-Tue 10.30am–2.30pm;
www.royalalberthall.com
The famous red-brick concert hall owes its reputation to the Proms, a series of classical music concerts held each summer, but it also stages pop, classical and jazz concerts.

SHOPPING

Harrods (**G** D1)
→ *Brompton Rd, SW1*
Tel. 020 7730 1234
Mon-Sat 10am–8pm;
Sun noon–6pm;
www.harrods.com
Founded by a tea merchant, Henry Charles Harrod in 1849, Harrods is London's most legendary store. The extraordinary Food Halls are the main attraction.

Harvey Nichols (**G** D1)
→ *109–125 Knightsbridge, SW1 Tel. 020 7235 5000*
Mon-Sat 10am–8pm;
Sun noon–6pm;
www.harveynichols.co.uk
'Harvey Nics', however, is London's most stylish department store and certainly has the edge on Harrods for designer collections. Popular sushi bar on the fifth floor.

The Pie Man (**G** D3)
→ *16 Cale St, Chelsea Green, SW3 Tel. 020 7225 0587*
Mon-Fri 9am–6pm;
Sat 9.30am–3pm
As an alternative to sandwiches, take out some of these delicious British dishes: lamb and mint pie, salmon cake or lemon cake.

King's Road
The whole of the King's Rd is lined with great shops: The Holding Company for leather baskets; the Designers' Guild for fabrics; L.K. Bennett for shoes, and:

Steinberg & Tolkien (**G** D3)
→ *193 King's Rd, SW3*
Tel. 020 7376 3660
Mon-Sat 11am–6.30pm;
Sun noon–6pm
Second-hand designer accessories and clothes worthy of a fashion museum. Hermès sweaters, Schiaparelli necklaces, and outfits by Chanel, Ossie Clark, Pucci, Westwood, etc.

Chelsea Farmers' Market (**G** C3)
→ *125 Sydney St, SW3*
A miniature market with an eclectic mix of stores in small, multicolored wooden huts.

Map F

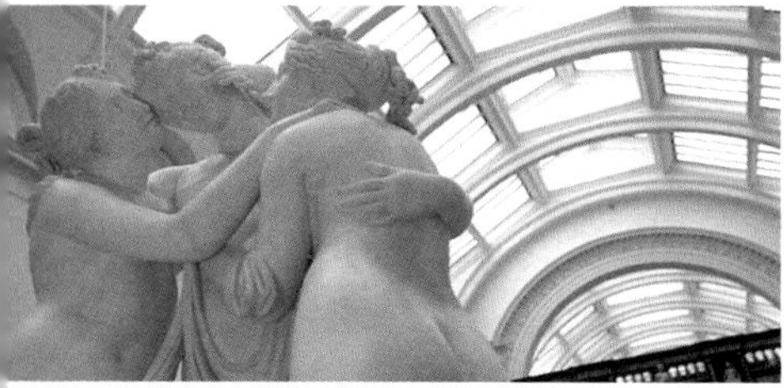

ORIA & ALBERT MUSEUM

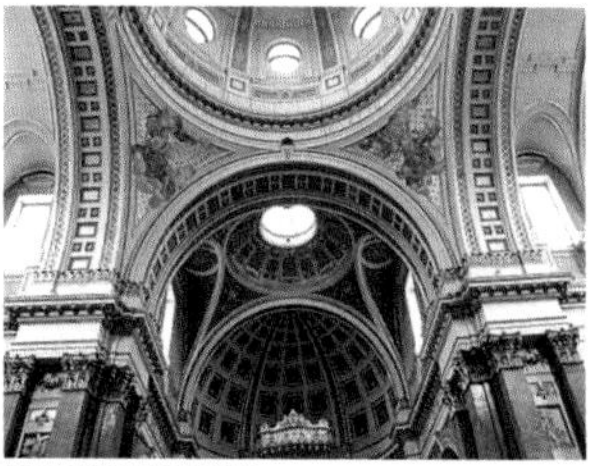

BROMPTON ORATORY

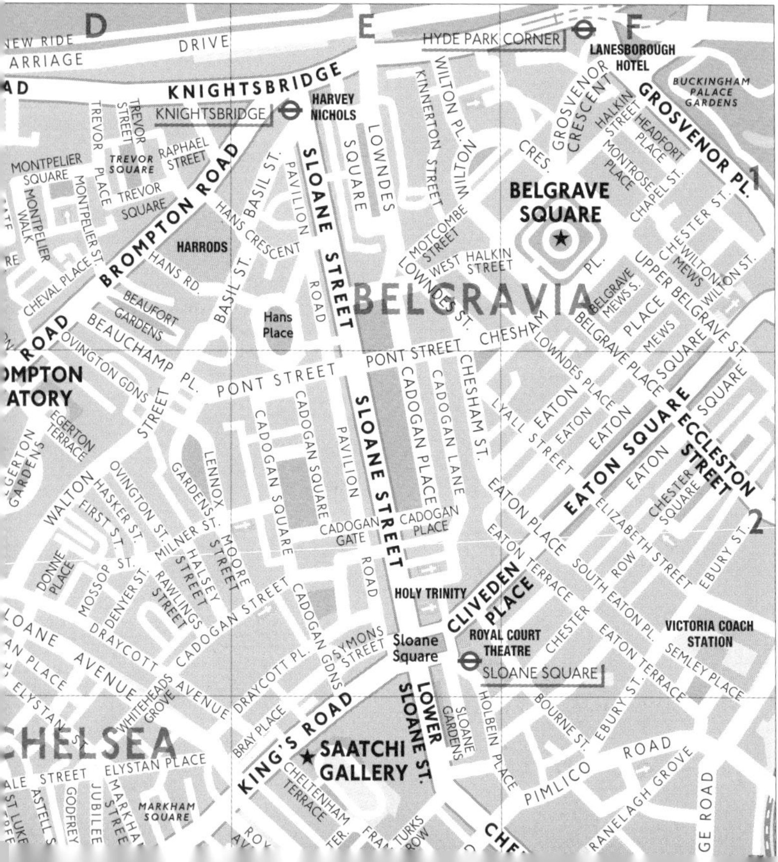
D
E
F
1
2
NEW RIDE
ARRIAGE
DRIVE
HYDE PARK CORNER
LANESBOROUGH HOTEL
BUCKINGHAM PALACE GARDENS
KNIGHTSBRIDGE
HARVEY NICHOLS
TREVOR STREET
TREVOR PLACE
RAPHAEL STREET
TREVOR SQUARE
MONTPELIER SQUARE
MONTPELIER WALK
MONTPELIER ST.
BROMPTON ROAD
HARRODS
HANS RD.
HANS CRESCENT
BASIL ST.
HANS PLACE
PAVILION ROAD
SLOANE STREET
LOWNDES SQUARE
KINNERTON STREET
WILTON PL.
WILTON CRESCENT
GROSVENOR CRESCENT
CRES.
HALKIN STREET
HEADFORT PLACE
MONTROSE PLACE
GROSVENOR PL.
CHAPEL ST.
BELGRAVE SQUARE
CHESTER ST.
WILTON MEWS
WILTON ST.
UPPER BELGRAVE
MOTCOMBE STREET
WEST HALKIN STREET
LOWNDES ST.
BELGRAVIA
BELGRAVE MEWS S.
PL.
CHEVAL PLACE
BEAUFORT GARDENS
BEAUCHAMP PL.
Hans Place
CHESHAM
LOWNDES PLACE
BELGRAVE PLACE
MEWS
BELGRAVE ST.
OVINGTON GDNS
MPTON ATORY
PONT STREET
CADOGAN PLACE
CADOGAN LANE
CHESHAM ST.
LYALL STREET
EATON
EATON SQUARE
ECCLESTON STREET
EGERTON TERRACE
EGERTON GARDENS
WALTON
HASKER ST.
FIRST ST.
OVINGTON ST.
MILNER ST.
LENNOX GARDENS
HALSEY STREET
MOORE STREET
CADOGAN SQUARE
CADOGAN GATE
EATON PLACE
CHESTER SQUARE
ELIZABETH STREET
EBURY ST.
DONNE PLACE
MOSSOP ST.
DENYER ST.
RAWLINGS STREET
CADOGAN STREET
HOLY TRINITY
CLIVEDEN PLACE
EATON TERRACE
SOUTH EATON PL.
ROW
VICTORIA COACH STATION
SLOANE AVENUE
DRAYCOTT AVENUE
ELYSTAN PLACE
SYMONS STREET
Sloane Square
ROYAL COURT THEATRE
SLOANE SQUARE
CHESTER
SEMLEY PLACE
WHITEHEADS GROVE
DRAYCOTT PL.
CADOGAN GDNS
LOWER SLOANE ST.
SLOANE GARDENS
HOLBEIN PLACE
BOURNE ST.
EBURY ST.
CHELSEA
BRAY PLACE
KING'S ROAD
SAATCHI GALLERY
PIMLICO ROAD
RANELAGH GROVE
ELYSTAN PLACE
STREET
GODFREY
JUBILEE
MARKHAM SQUARE
CHELTENHAM TERRACE
TURKS ROW
→ Map A

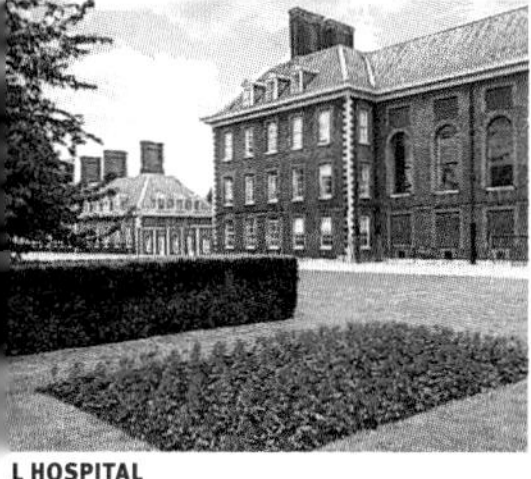
L HOSPITAL

CHELSEA PHYSIC GARDEN

CHEYNE WALK

·20 7808 0900
·7am–8pm
Baroque Catholic
·ch (1804) houses
·atues of the apostles
·azzuoli (1644–1725)
h once stood in the
·edral in Siena, Italy.
·tchi Gallery (G F3)
·ng's Rd, Duke of York's
·W3 Tel. 020 7823 2363
10am–8pm (10pm
·t); www.saatchi-
·ry.co.uk
·art collection of the
·wned and controversial
·es Saatchi moved from
·ty Hall to these
·tiful premises in 2007.
·gallery's mission is to
·ort British modern art
·exhibits artists such as Tracey Emin, Damien Hirst, Sarah Lucas, Duane Hanson, the Chapman brothers and more.

★ Belgrave Square (G F1)
The haunt of robbers before it was developed, this very orderly district was designed in 1820 by Thomas Cubitt. Beautifully proportioned brick and white stuccoed Victorian buildings, so typical of Chelsea, border the square.

★ Royal Hospital (G E3)
→ Royal Hospital Rd, SW3 Tel. 020 7881 5200 Daily 10am–noon, 2–4pm; gardens: daily 10am (noon Sun)–8.30pm (4.30pm Nov-March; 7pm April & Sep; 5pm Oct)
The famous Chelsea Flower Show is held in May in the gardens of this army retirement home founded by Charles II in the 17th century. Its 400 Chelsea Pensioners, in 18th-century uniform, wear a tricorn hat on special occasions. The chapel and refectory are open to visitors.

★ Chelsea Physic Garden (G E4)
→ 66 Royal Hospital Rd, SW3 Tel. 020 7352 5646 April-Oct: Tue-Fri noon–5pm (sunset Wed); Sun noon–6pm
The oldest botanical garden in England, along with that of Oxford, the Chelsea Physic Garden was founded in 1673 by the Apothecaries' Company, which wanted medicinal plants for scientific study. Through the centuries the garden grew more exotic species, thanks to gifts by, most notably, Sir Hans Sloane. Today there are more than 7,000 varieties of herbs, fruits and vegetables, and many centenary trees.

★ Cheyne Walk (G D4)
The Pre-Raphaelite Brotherhood was founded at no. 16; Henry James lived at no. 21; George Elliot died at no. 4, and J. W. M. Turner at no. 119. These are just a few of the famous names who occupied the elegant Georgian townhouses of the pretty Cheyne Walk, which runs alongside the river.

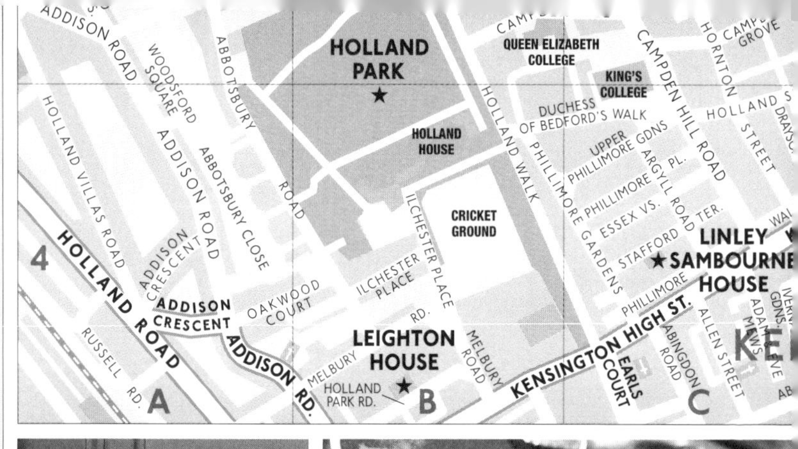

LINLEY SAMBOURNE HOUSE

KENSINGTON PALACE

★ **Portobello Market** (**H** B2)
→ *Portobello & Golborne rds Mon-Sat 8am–7pm*
This huge market is a must on Saturdays when fruit and vegetable stalls jostle for space with stalls selling antiques, second-hand clothes and bric-a-brac.

★ **Notting Hill** (**H** A2)
At night the pubs in Westbourne Park Road act as a magnet for the young and trendy, the stars and starlets, and of couse the locals. Notting Hill, a somewhat neglected district until the 1990s, became popular with young wealthy professionals hungry for a more diverse, Bohemian atmosphere. Georgian houses stand on the higher ground, streets on the slopes are lined with pastel houses and more dilapidated districts extend further north. Over the last weekend in August a million people throng the streets for a spectacular fancy-dress parade and festival, organized by the area's West Indian residents since the 1960s.

★ **Holland Park** (**H** B4)
Daily 8am–9pm
The most romantic and densely wooded of London's parks comprises a group of small gardens (the Dutch, Rose, Iris and Japanese gardens) which are home to strutting peacocks. All that remains of Holland House (1607), the Dutch-style manor house to which these lands once belonged, is the west wing, a rare vestige of the Jacobean period. On summer evenings plays, ballets and operas are performed on the terrace. The park also has a gourmet restaurant, The Belvedere (see previous page), and a café.

★ **Kensington Palace** (**H** D3)
→ *Kensington Gardens, W8 Tel. 0870 751 5176 Daily 10am–6pm (5pm Nov-Feb)*
In 1689, King William III, afflicted with asthma, decided to take advant of Kensington's pure ai He asked Christopher Wren and Nicholas Hawksmoor to enlarge existing brick and white stone manor house anc turn it into a royal residence. Between 16 and 1837 all the British rulers lived and died he Princess Victoria was baptized in the Cupola Room in 1819 and held her first privy council in the Red Saloon on the she ascended the thror The apartments are resplendent with oak paneling, trompe-l'œil designs on the ceilings walls, portraits of mem

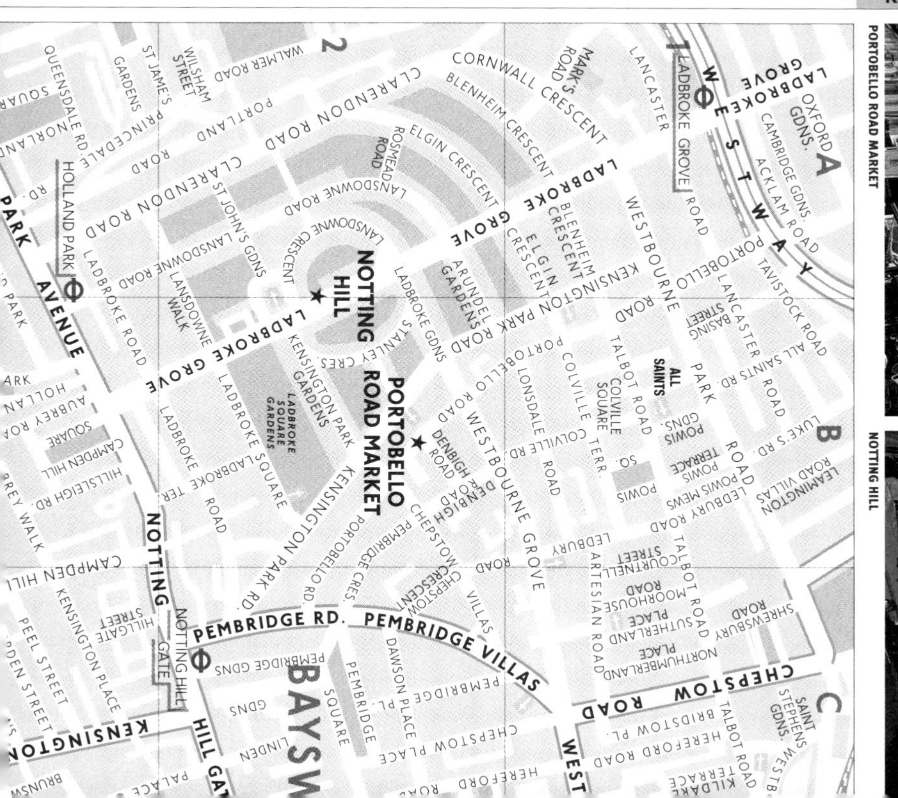

PORTOBELLO ROAD MARKET

NOTTING HILL

Kensington, a holiday resort on the outskirts of the city even before Kensington Palace became the royal residence in 1689, still has a split personality. It is both a busy shopping center, with its many stores on Kensington High Street, and a prestigious residential area made up of stately houses and converted mews buildings. The influx of wealthy professionals and celebrities to the north of Notting Hill Gate has scotched Notting Hill's erstwhile reputation as a ghetto. A sensational carnival is organized at the end of every August by the African and West-Indian community living to the east and north of Portobello Road.

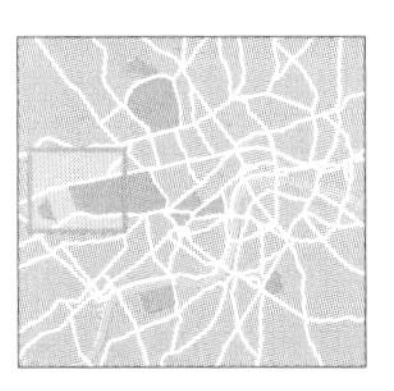

WAGAMAMA

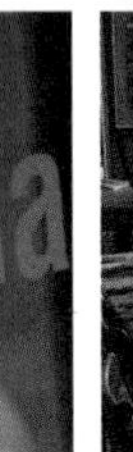

MAGGIE JONES

RESTAURANTS

Wagamama (**H** D4)
→ *26 Kensington High St, W8 Tel. 020 7376 1717 Daily noon–11pm (10pm Sun)*
Wagamama was the first eatery of its kind when it appeared in the 1990s: wooden benches, shared tables in a canteen-style space, good Japanese noodle dishes. Simple, healthy food for around £12 per head. Other branches throughout London.

Costa's (**H** C3)
→ *18 Hillgate St, W8 Tel. 020 7727 4310 Tue-Sat noon–2.30pm, 6–10.30pm*
Generous portions of fresh fish & chips, squid, scampi, fishcakes and the like. Eat in or take out for a modest price. £10.

The Cow (**H** C1)
→ *89 Westbourne Park Rd, W2 Tel. 020 7221 0021 Mon-Sat noon–4pm, 6–11pm; Sun 12.30–3.30pm, 7–10pm*
A trendy Notting Hill hangout, The Cow is a relaxed, friendly Irish bar downstairs, serving fresh oysters and Guinness, and a relaxed gastropub upstairs, with an accent on seafood (lobster linguine, smoked trout). Carte £15–20 (upstairs).

Maggie Jones (**H** D4)
→ *6 Old Court Place, W8 Tel. 020 7937 6462 Daily 12.30–2.30pm, 6.30–11pm*
An unexpected and welcome haven behind the busy Kensington High St. This three-story restaurant looks like an old farmhouse, with wooden floorboards, snug nooks and crannies, and old wine bottles serving as candle holders. Simple British fare: steak and kidney pie, corn on the cob with nutmeg mayonnaise, fish pie. Lovely staff and a very romantic atmosphere at dinner. £20–25.

The Belvedere (**H** B4)
→ *Holland Park, next to the car park off Abbotsbury Rd, W8 Tel. 020 7602 1238 Daily noon–2.30pm, 6–11pm; closed Sun dinner*
An oasis of elegance and tranquillity in the heart of Holland Park, with parquet floors, high-ceilinged windows and small round tables looking out onto greenery. There's also a magnificent terrace to eat al fresco in summer, but it has few tables so reserve ahead. Unpretentious, delicious modern British cuisine. Three-course weekend set lunch £25. Carte £17–30.

RCHILL ARMS

THE SPICE SHOP

URBAN OUTFITTERS

TEAROOM

The Orangery (**H** D3)
→ *Kensington Palace, Kensington Gardens, W8*
Tel. 020 7376 0239
Daily 10am–6pm
Experience traditional high tea (scones, jams and sandwiches) in this large, light and airy greenhouse, designed by Sir John Vanbrugh for Queen Anne in 1704.

BARS, PUBS, MOVIE THEATER

Ladbroke Arms (**H** B2)
→ *54 Ladbroke Rd, W11*
Tel. 020 7727 6648
Mon-Sat 11am–11pm; Sun noon–10.30pm
Welcoming pub in a little yellow house, with open fires, comfy maroon seats and a terrace. It has in recent years also started serving very good food.

Churchill Arms (**H** C3)
→ *119 Kensington Church St, W8 Tel. 020 7727 4242*
Mon-Sat 11am–11pm (midnight Thu-Sat); Sun noon–10.30pm
The walls and ceilings of this large pub are hung with countless objects: wicker baskets, copper utensils, butterflies, paintings, photographs. Very popular both for its atmosphere and for the excellent and cheap Thai food – so you may find it hard to get a table.

Julie's Wine Bar (**H** A3)
→ *135 Portland Rd, W11*
Tel. 020 7727 7985 Daily 9am–11pm (10.30pm Sun)
One of the most romantic places to have a drink in London (it is also a very good restaurant). A haven of calm, several minutes' walk from Portobello Rd market. Sit on the shady terrace or step inside where, over two floors, alcoves form Andalusian-style lounges with plants and some fine oriental touches to the decor.

Electric Cinema (**H** B2)
→ *191 Portobello Rd, W11*
Tel. 020 7908 9696
A mythical movie theater (and the first in London, dating from 1911) it was entirely refurbished in 2002. Coming to see a movie here is a special and comfortable experience – leather seating or two-seater sofas with footstools, side tables for food and drink, snack bar. Mainstream and art house programs. The Electric Brasserie next door, open for breakfast, lunch and dinner, is recommended.

SHOPPING

Blenheim Crescent (**H** A1)

→ Books for Cooks *(no. 4)*
Tel. 020 7221 1992
Mon-Sat 9.30am–6pm; Sun 11am–4pm
Cook books from floor to ceiling and a tiny eatery which tries out recipes from some of the volumes on sale.

→ Travel Bookshop *(no. 13)*
Tel. 020 7229 5260
Mon-Sat 10am–6pm
As featured in the *Notting Hill* movie. Travel books from floor to ceiling.

→ The Spice Shop *(no. 1)*
Tel. 020 7221 4448
Mon-Sat 9.30am–6pm; Sun 11am–3pm
The bright yellow shop front conceals an Ali-Baba's cave of treasures: dried fruit, aromatic herbs and spices etc.

→ Ceramica Blue *(no. 10)*
Tel. 020 7727 0288
Mon-Sat 10am–6.30pm; Sun noon–5pm; www.ceramicablue.co.uk
The tableware, tiles and giftware on offer here are the work of 20 potters from different countries. Super colors and craftsmanship.

Urban Outfitters (**H** D4)
→ *36 Kensington High St, W8 Tel. 020 7761 1001*
Mon-Sat 10am–7pm (8pm Thu); Sun noon–6pm
This immense concrete space is filled with an organized chaos of cards, fashionable clothes, household objects, accessories and magazines. Beautiful rugs with stylized flowers, fun shower curtains and fancy candles. Several branches in London.

202 - Nicole Farhi (**H** B2)
→ *202 Westbourne Grove, W11 Tel. 020 7792 6888*
Mon 10am–6pm; Tue-Sat 8.30am–6pm; Sun 10am–5pm
A concept store by Nicole Farhi, part fashionable café, part fashion store. It stocks women's and children's clothes, objets d'art and accessories the designer found while traveling around the world.

Paul Smith (**H** B2)
→ *Westbourne House, 122 Kensington Park Rd, W11*
Tel. 020 7727 3553
Mon-Sat 10am–6pm (6.30pm Sat)
Magnificent shop with collections for men, women and children by one of the stars of English fashion. Materials with exquisite patterns and colors are combined with classic cuts and retro or ethnic touches.

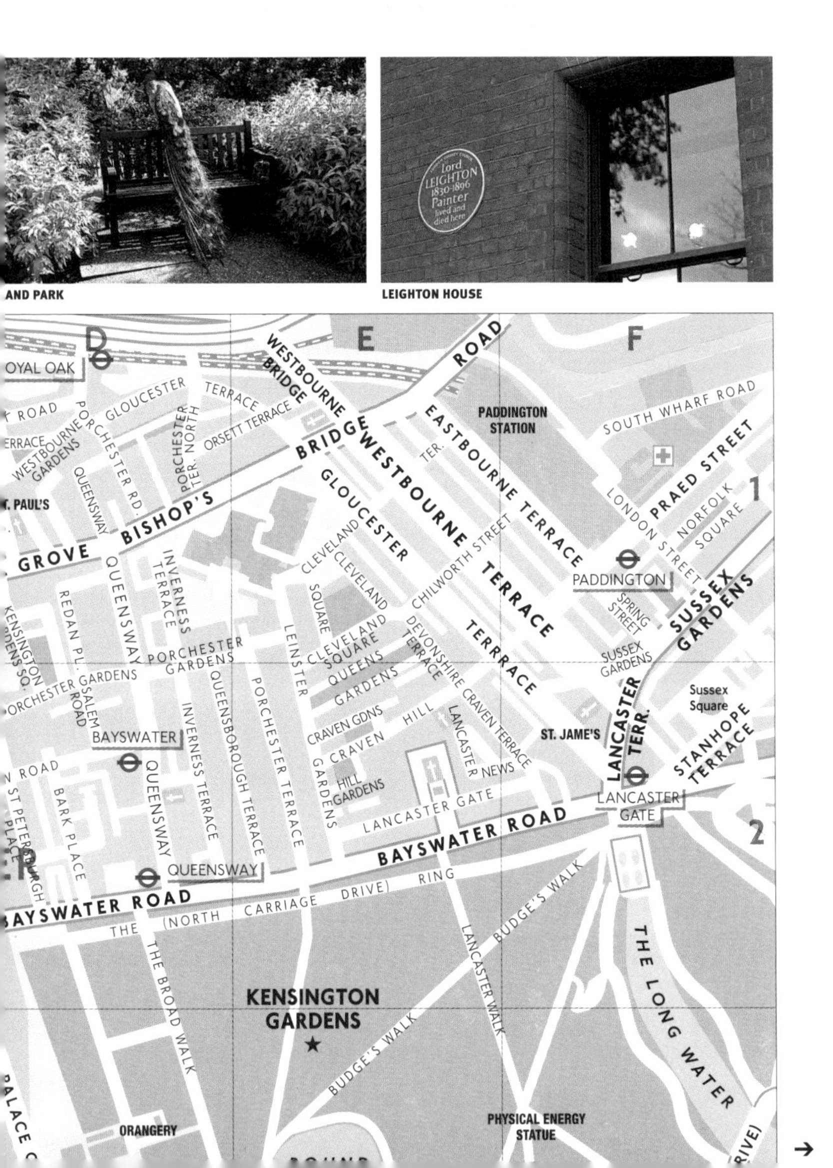
AND PARK
Lord
LEIGHTON
1830-1896
Painter
lived and
died here
LEIGHTON HOUSE
D
E
F
1
2
OYAL OAK
GLOUCESTER TERRACE
PORCHESTER TER. NORTH
ORSETT TERRACE
WESTBOURNE BRIDGE
ROAD
PADDINGTON STATION
SOUTH WHARF ROAD
WESTBOURNE GARDENS
PORCHESTER RD.
QUEENSWAY
BRIDGE
WESTBOURNE
EASTBOURNE TERRACE
TER.
PRAED STREET
LONDON STREET
NORFOLK SQUARE
T. PAUL'S
BISHOP'S
GLOUCESTER
CHILWORTH STREET
GROVE
INVERNESS TERRACE
CLEVELAND
CLEVELAND SQUARE
TERRACE
PADDINGTON
SPRING STREET
SUSSEX GARDENS
KENSINGTON GARDENS SQ.
REDAN PL.
QUEENSWAY
PORCHESTER GARDENS
LEINSTER
CLEVELAND SQUARE
QUEENS GARDENS
DEVONSHIRE TERRACE
TERRRACE
SUSSEX GARDENS
PORCHESTER GARDENS
SALEM ROAD
INVERNESS TERRACE
QUEENSBOROUGH TERRACE
PORCHESTER TERRACE
CRAVEN GDNS
HILL
LANCASTER
CRAVEN TERRACE
Sussex Square
BAYSWATER
CRAVEN
ST. JAME'S
LANCASTER TERR.
STANHOPE TERRACE
ROAD
GARDENS
HILL GARDENS
NEWS
ST PETERSBURGH PLACE
BARK PLACE
QUEENSWAY
LANCASTER GATE
LANCASTER GATE
BAYSWATER ROAD
QUEENSWAY
RING
BAYSWATER ROAD
THE (NORTH CARRIAGE DRIVE)
BUDGE'S WALK
LANCASTER WALK
THE BROAD WALK
THE LONG WATER
KENSINGTON GARDENS
BUDGE'S WALK
PALACE
ORANGERY
PHYSICAL ENERGY STATUE
RIVE)
→

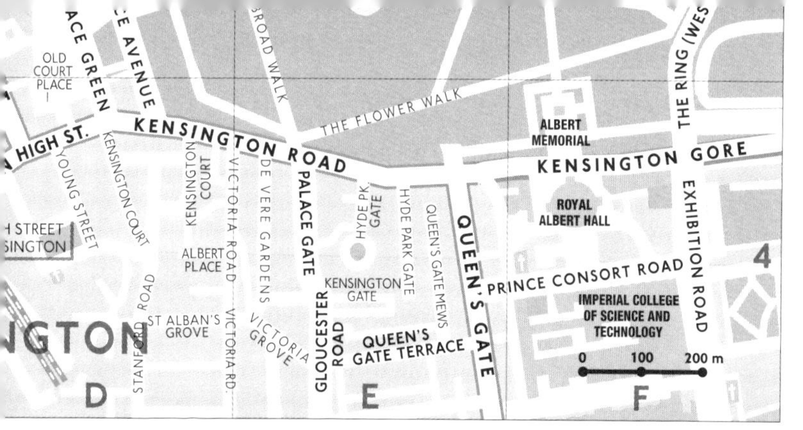

INGTON GARDENS

SERPENTINE GALLERY

e royal family and
urniture which once
nged to them.

nley Sambourne
se (H C4)
' *Stafford Terrace, W8*
020 7602 3316
s by appointment
ntly reopened after
r restoration work.
was the home,
een 1874 and 1946,
mbourne, an
rator of the satirical
azine *Punch* and a
orter of the Arts and
s movement which
d to emulate the
y of traditional
s and techniques.
culously, the
rian interior is virtually unchanged. Most of the decorative elements in the house, including the original wallpaper, are by William Morris.

★ Leighton House (H B4)
→ *12 Holland Park Rd, W14*
Tel. 020 7602 3316
Wed-Mon 11am–5.30pm
Extravagance reigns supreme behind the classical façade. Frederick Lord Leighton, artist and president of the Royal Academy, was a keen traveler and orientalist. He wanted red walls in the style of a Venetian palace, and an Arab hall worthy of an Eastern palace. The house had everything, including faïence tiles from Iznik and the gentle murmur of a fountain. Also on display is a wonderful collection of pre-Raphaelite paintings by Leighton's friends, particularly canvases by Burne-Jones and Millais.

★ Kensington Gardens (H E3)
→ *Daily 6am–sunset*
This park, originally a playground for the nation's young queens, is now a children's paradise with model boats sailing on the Round Pond, a statue of Peter Pan, puppet shows in the summer and two playgrounds. The flower beds and water features in the Sunken Gardens, hidden by the foliage of lime trees, are reminiscent of Tudor gardens.

Serpentine Gallery (H F3)
→ *Kensington Gardens, W2*
Tel. 020 7402 6075
Daily 10am–6pm
A lovely tea pavilion (1934) surrounded by greenery, which was turned into an art gallery in 1970 and stages exhibitions of, and special events relating to, modern and contemporary art. Man Ray, Henry Moore, Andy Warhol, Bridget Riley, Damien Hirst and Rachel Whiteread are just a few of the artists who have exhibited here.

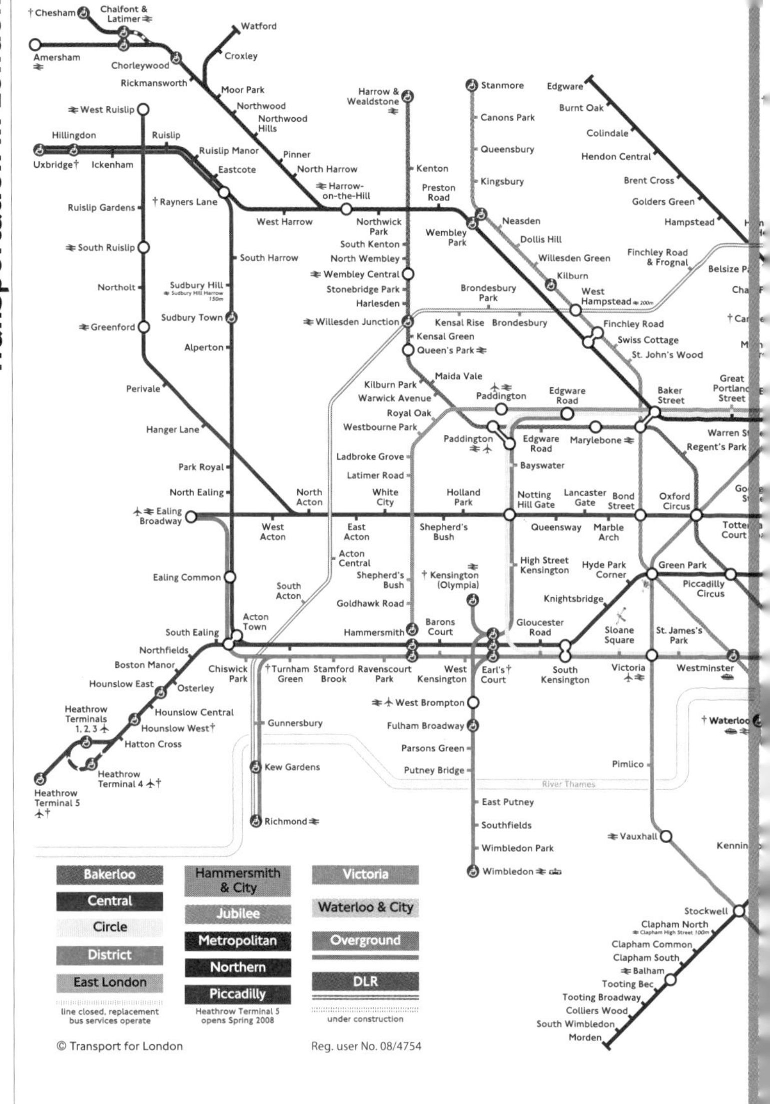

MAYOR OF LONDON

24 hour travel information
020 7222 1234

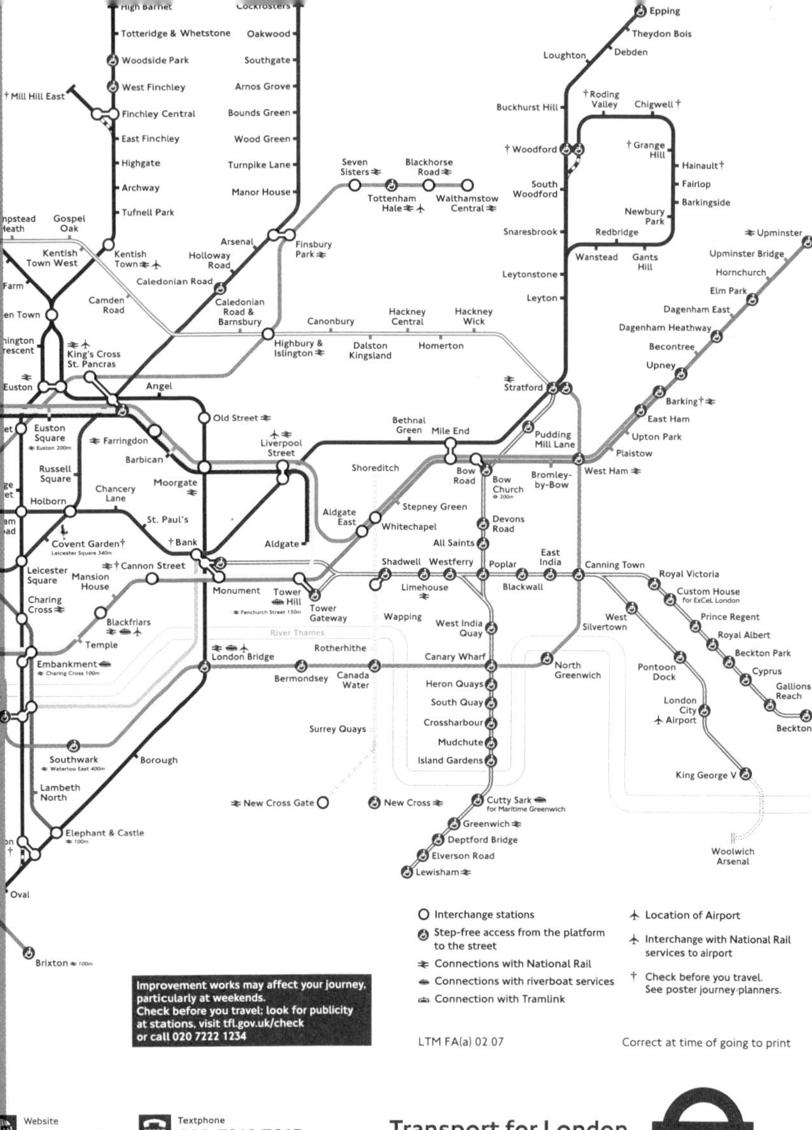

High Barnet
Totteridge & Whetstone
Woodside Park
West Finchley
Mill Hill East
Finchley Central
East Finchley
Highgate
Archway
Tufnell Park
Cockfosters
Oakwood
Southgate
Arnos Grove
Bounds Green
Wood Green
Turnpike Lane
Manor House
Seven Sisters
Tottenham Hale
Blackhorse Road
Walthamstow Central
Epping
Theydon Bois
Debden
Loughton
Buckhurst Hill
Roding Valley
Chigwell
Woodford
Grange Hill
Hainault
Fairlop
Barkingside
Newbury Park
South Woodford
Snaresbrook
Redbridge
Wanstead
Gants Hill
Leytonstone
Leyton
Upminster
Upminster Bridge
Hornchurch
Elm Park
Dagenham East
Dagenham Heathway
Becontree
Upney
Barking
East Ham
Upton Park
Plaistow
West Ham
Gospel Oak
Kentish Town West
Kentish Town
Camden Road
Holloway Road
Arsenal
Finsbury Park
Caledonian Road
Caledonian Road & Barnsbury
Canonbury
Hackney Central
Hackney Wick
Highbury & Islington
Dalston Kingsland
Homerton
King's Cross St. Pancras
Euston
Angel
Old Street
Euston Square
Euston 200m
Farringdon
Barbican
Russell Square
Moorgate
Liverpool Street
Bethnal Green
Mile End
Stratford
Pudding Mill Lane
Bow Road
Bow Church
200m
Bromley-by-Bow
Shoreditch
Stepney Green
Chancery Lane
Holborn
St. Paul's
Covent Garden
Leicester Square 340m
Bank
Aldgate East
Whitechapel
Aldgate
Devons Road
All Saints
Leicester Square
Mansion House
Cannon Street
Monument
Tower Hill
Fenchurch Street 150m
Tower Gateway
Shadwell
Westferry
Limehouse
Poplar
East India
Blackwall
Canning Town
Royal Victoria
Custom House for ExCeL London
Prince Regent
Royal Albert
Beckton Park
Cyprus
Gallions Reach
Beckton
Charing Cross
Blackfriars
Temple
Wapping
West India Quay
West Silvertown
River Thames
Embankment
Charing Cross 100m
London Bridge
Rotherhithe
Canary Wharf
North Greenwich
Pontoon Dock
London City Airport
Bermondsey
Canada Water
Heron Quays
South Quay
Crossharbour
Mudchute
Island Gardens
Surrey Quays
Southwark
Waterloo East 400m
Borough
Lambeth North
King George V
New Cross Gate
New Cross
Cutty Sark for Maritime Greenwich
Greenwich
Deptford Bridge
Elverson Road
Lewisham
Woolwich Arsenal
Elephant & Castle
100m
Oval
Brixton 100m
Interchange stations
Step-free access from the platform to the street
Connections with National Rail
Connections with riverboat services
Connection with Tramlink
Location of Airport
Interchange with National Rail services to airport
Check before you travel. See poster journey planners.
Improvement works may affect your journey, particularly at weekends. Check before you travel; look for publicity at stations, visit tfl.gov.uk/check or call 020 7222 1234
LTM FA(a) 02.07
Correct at time of going to print

Website
tfl.gov.uk

Textphone
020 7918 3015

Transport for London

The names of streets, monuments and places to visit are listed alphabetically. They are followed by one or several map references (**F** A3), whose first letter in bold refers to the corresponding area and map.

Streets